SOUTH WALES

Edited by Simon Harwin

First published in Great Britain in 1999 by
YOUNG WRITERS
Remus House,
Coltsfoot Drive,
Woodston,
Peterborough, PE2 9JX
Telephone (01733) 890066

HB ISBN 0 75431 672 6
SB ISBN 0 75431 673 4

FOREWORD

Young Writers have produced poetry books in conjunction with schools for over eight years; providing a platform for talented young people to shine. This year, the Celebration 2000 collection of regional anthologies were developed with the millennium in mind.

With the nation taking stock of how far we have come, and reflecting on what we want to achieve in the future, our anthologies give a vivid insight into the thoughts and experiences of the younger generation.

We were once again impressed with the quality and attention to detail of every entry received and hope you will enjoy the poems we have decided to feature in *Celebration 2000 South Wales* for many years to come.

CONTENTS

Cwmllynfell Primary School

Groes Primary School

Gwaunfarren Primary School

Leigh Price	51
Stephen Thomas	52
Rhydian Gareth Patterson	52
Bethan Jones	53
Lee Greenaway	54
Jonathan Thomas	54
Hana Imiolczyk	55
Keith Phillips	55
Marie Louise Morgans	56
Tara Jones	56
Lois Dale Jenkins	57
Daniel Foley	57
Christian Evans	58
Craig Rhys Barlow	58
Sarah Ford	59
James Cushen	60

Hendre Junior School

Hannah Stokes	60
Jonathan Rees	60
Jamie Jackson	61
Rachel McCarthy	61
Ryan David Forehead	62
Bechan Carpenter	62
Richard Kestell	63
Rachel Davies	63
Verity Davies	64
Jenna Swan	64
Laura McKinty	65
Bethan Newbury	65
Stacey Spargo	66
Kadie Louise Ruck	66
Danielle Wood	67
Gemma Morgan & Lindsey Jones	67
Dane Hutton	68
Charlotte Harper	68
Rebecca Mannings	68

Daniel Jones	69
Blaine Harrington	69
Laura Davies	70
Arianna Willetts	70
Sarah Giurani	71
Christopher Hutchings	71
Laura Jenkins	72

Jenner Park Primary School

Melissa Brown	72
Thomas Davie	73
Nicholas James	73
Michael Jenkins	74
Matthew Selby	74
Scott Jones	75
Rhian John	75
Logan Saunders	76
Ellis Mazey	76
Holly Miller	77
Louis John Ayres	77
Michelle Green	78
Sian Jones	78
Michael Cundliffe	79
Shaun Newman	79
Kyle Haggarty	80
Stacey Pope	80
Michael Osborne	81
Christopher Burston	81
Nicole Kear	82
Abbey Rowlands	82
Mary Doyle	83
Sylvia Doyle	83
Samantha Germon & Tabitha Brown	84
Peter Pearce	84
Mark Michael Gronow	85
Laura J Hawkins	85

Luke Matthews	86
Michelle Stanton	87
Dawn Baker	87
Kyle Wheeler-Adams	88

Mayhill Junior School

Jamie Elsworth	89
Kimberley L Pearce	89

Overmonnow Primary School

Luke Frost	90

Park Terrace Primary School

Rebecca Jones	90
Jade Charles	91
Gemma Blake	92
Eleanor Harris	92
Nisha Evans-Derrick	93

Pen-y-Fro Primary School

Jason Rees	93
Felix Morgan	94
Geraint Davies	94
Abi Carroll	95
Robert Kirkhouse	95
Amy Griffiths	96
Charlotte Jones	96
Charlie Foulkes	97
Rhys Smith	97
Oliver Corbisiero	98
Heather Mills	98
Lara Amber Roberts	99
Ria Davies	100

St Alban's RC Primary School, Pontypool

Kristy Jones	100
Laura Bisset	101
Lisa Bisset	102

Tutshill CE Primary School

Richard Clarke	155
Kaylee Bains	155
Chloe Martin	156
Katie Smith	156
Kelly Duncan	157
Robert Jones	158
Sophie McRoberts	158
Kristina Ellen Connolly	159
Harriet Lewis	159
Tristesse Hawker	160
Tommy Edwards	160
Lyndsey Connolly	161
Ashvin Nair	161
Heather Leighton	162
Aimee Townshend	162
Tristan Truran	163
Katie Szmaglik	163
Justin Fisher	164
Amy Beavis	164
Rebecca Goatman	165
Lucy Stewart	166
Philip Simpson	166
Heather Cameron	167
Christopher Williams	167
Sarah Bradley	168
Serena Corbin	168
Natasha Cubbin	169
Jessica Hollies	169
Freya Mills	170
Gemma Duncan	170
Alice Workman	171
Sarah Parsons	171
Alex Compton	172
Matthew Newell	172
Alex Pritchard	173
Emma Childs	173
Rosalind Jacks	174

The Poems

THE THINGS I LOVE

A rich, sweet chocolate cake,
A gentle boat ride on a peaceful lake,
The blazing, fiery sun in the sky,
A battered football flying by,
A gigantic bowl of warm pasta,
Maybe a day without the headmaster!
With a sparkler spinning and writing my name,
What about tennis, just a friendly game!
A giggle with my friend late at night,
A gallery of art, what a beautiful sight!
The autumn leaves cover the grounds,
A deep, dark forest with its mysterious sounds,
The cold, crisp snow disguising the land,
A beach with its beautiful sea and sand,
The sun moving out of sight,
Followed by the moon of the dark night!

Katie Haines (11)

THE STORM

Sky darkening,
Hailstones stinging,
Jumping, shooting.
Lightening flashing,
Thunder drumming,
Crashing, banging.
Rain splashing,
Wind blowing,
Howling, twirling.
The storm is growing.

Jonathan Daniel Durbin (9)
Blaen-y-Maes Primary School

THE SPELL

Take a wing of a bat,
Take a tail of a cat,
Take an eye of a rat,
Put them in a witch's hat,
Boil them, fry them, stir them
And so that is that.

Stacey Shoemake (10)
Blaen-y-Maes Primary School

FIREWORKS

I saw fireworks
Shooting in the sky,
Twisting, twirling, whirling,
Swirling, spinning, zooming,
Whizzing, dancing, prancing
And crashing into life.

Stuart Stokes (9)
Blaen-y-Maes Primary School

FRED

There was an old monster called Fred
Who couldn't get out of bed.
He slept all night
So they gave him a fright
By pouring water over his head.

Karl Davies (10)
Blaen-y-Maes Primary School

ACROSTIC POEM

G randma was invented by Roald Dahl
R evolting, rigid and rude
A n acrid, dirty demon who's
N ever ever in a good mood.
D elicious things like cake she turns away
M eal of rotten maggots for tea and dinner today,
A nd don't forget the worms with mashed slugs she said.

Kayleigh Thomas (10)
Blaen-y-Maes Primary School

THE WIND

I am the wind, I am strong,
I don't think I am wrong.
When I blow I have a riot
And after I am quiet.
Sometimes when I blow I can harm
But sometimes I can be calm.

Stacey French (8)
Blaen-y-Maes Primary School

WITCHES

Hissing, fissing witches brew
Stir it up into a stew
Bubbling, hubbling, sloshing, sploshing
Oh Grandma if you only knew
What a stew I've made for you.

Michelle Goosey (11)
Blaen-y-Maes Primary School

CRY IN THE NIGHT

What could it be?
That cry in the night.
Whatever it was
It gave me a fright.

There in the woods
I stood alone
I heard someone
Give a groan.

I turned around
But no one was there.
Whatever it was
It gave me a scare.

Donna Hammond (11)
Blaen-y-Maes Primary School

THE FISHING TRIP

A beautiful day to go fishing
What will the day bring to me?
A perch, a carp, a tiny gudgeon?
Fishing's the life for me.

Loop line through eye and weight and hook
Tied on with a fisherman's knot.
Maggots on hook, they're squirming a lot,
Ready to cast into the brook.

Sit on my tackle box waiting,
Waiting to see my float sink.
Strike, reel-in, what will it bring?
It's a silvery perch for me.

Scott Travis (9)
Clydach Primary School

SWEET DREAMS

Dancing in a palace made of teeth,
Little children sleep beneath,
Glittered by their sleeping dust,
For happy faces is a must.
Slender feet tiptoe your pillow,
Others wait beneath the willow,
Hushed laughter of delight
While awaiting in the night
For the present she'll retrieve,
The tooth you left, for you believe!
Her feathered dress brushes past your cheek
As your deepest sleep is at its peak,
Golden crowns glitter in street lights
Unnoticed by the cloak of night.

Jade Stoner (9)
Clydach Primary School

MY BOAT

My boat adrift on the sea,
And the boat's captain is me.
So cold it feels like snowing,
A gentle breeze blowing.
I'm sitting by the windowpane,
And I'm daydreaming again.
My muffler wrapped round my neck,
Some men sitting upon the deck.

David Bowkett (10)
Clydach Primary School

MY DOG

My dog is big,
       black,
       furry,
       happy,
       waggy,
My dog can fly over the gate
to meet me when I am late.
He is a friend to me,
and takes me for a walk.
My dog is as big as Loch Ness,
his kennel is always a mess.

Zoe Lynch (10)
Clydach Primary School

THE MILLENNIUM

All the people in the world
Are saying 'Yes the future's here.'
Children laugh,
Parents cheer,
What's so special about this year?
New adventures,
New beginnings,
New horizons,
Children singing,
Firework parties, lots of fun,
The new millennium has begun.

Paul Travis (11)
Clydach Primary School

THE WEATHER

The sun is a golden pearl,
Shining, shimmering all day long,
Glistening so brightly,
The ray's are so hot.

The rain splashes down on the ground,
Splosh, splash, splosh, splash,
Pitter-patter on the ground,
Sparkling as it's coming down.

The clouds are so fluffy,
All cosy and white,
Floating along the sky,
Reflecting on a deep, blue ocean.

Sleet is so slushy and wet,
Turning into puddles,
Making the ground so watery,
Shedding water all around.

Snow is as gentle,
Melting in your hands,
Spreading over lands,
Leaving a sheet of white.

The rainbow is so colourful,
Showing off its radiant colours,
Making everything so bright,
A painting of so many colours.

Weather is just weather.

Kate Pritchard (10)
Clydach Primary School

My Family

My sister, my sister is three years old,
She crawls and she falls,
She shouts and screams.
My sister, my sister I am fed up with my sister.

My brother, my brother is four years old,
He is as noisy as a monkey in a tree.
My brother, my brother I am very fed up with my brother.

My dad, my dad shouts and shouts but I
don't care 'cause inside's what counts.

My mum, my mum can't stop talking or walking.
My mum, my mum, I love my mum.

That's my family.

Emma Meredith (9)
Clydach Primary School

Furby

My Furby has a mind of its own,
It does all kinds of things when it's alone,
It talks and it walks and it runs around,
It flies high far from the ground,
My Furby is my greatest friend,
Our friendship will never ever end.

Lauren Thomas (10)
Clydach Primary School

WHAT IS THE MOON...?

The moon is a smile that God is
giving to people on the earth below.
The moon is a wave turning in the
sea, splashing the fish.
The moon is a handle on a dustbin
with the rubbish on the earth
below.
The moon is a bridge leading to
heaven.
The moon is the iron man's ear
trying to listen.
It brightens up the world.

Michael McShane (8)
Coed y Brain Primary School

WHAT IS THE MOON...?

The moon is a boat sailing on the sea.
The moon is a banana floating in space.
The moon is half a circle above our planet.
The moon is a crocodile's nose sneaking
through the water.
The moon is a ladder so God can come down.
The moon is a dog's tail wagging happily.

Matthew Walker (8)
Coed y Brain Primary School

A BEAUTIFUL BONFIRE

Bang, crackle, boom
on bonfire night.
I can see blazing patterns,
red, yellow, green, blue.
They sound like dishes smashing,
cutlery clanging.
They sound like wheels spinning,
metal breaking, bells ringing,
bombs dropping, people screaming.
It smells like wood burning,
chimneys smoking, chairs burning.
It looks like fire blazing,
trees waving,
colourful chalks in the sky.
The wind blows fireworks
round in circles.
People go home with smiling faces.
I like bonfire night -
Bang, crackle, *boom!*

Charlotte Lewis (8)
Coed y Brain Primary School

THE TRAIN

The train goes fast,
Faster than a cheetah or an aeroplane.
I see farmers getting crops out of the ground,
Horses running around a field.
I see a little boy riding on his bike,
And a sheepdog rounding up the sheep.

Luke Humphries (9)
Coed y Brain Primary School

THE SOLAR SYSTEM

Out in space,
stands the boss
controlling the speed and light of his people.
As they all go round him at their own natural speed,
the nine planets orbit the sun carrying their own
special message, passing it on,
to a planet named Pluto
who takes it to the stars
which follows the simple instructions.
Pluto goes back to receive another message
and the cycle continues
with the boss watching
time after time.

David Saunders (11)
Coed y Brain Primary School

THE MOON

The moon is a grey marble
that stands still in the sky.

The moon is a crumpled up
piece of paper in the bin.

The moon is a light bulb
flashing on and off.

The moon is a rock floating
in space.

The moon is a glass ball
thrown high in the sky.

Adam Beecham (7)
Coed y Brain Primary School

AUTUMN

As autumn starts
The conkers shine
And fall off trees.

The nights get colder,
The nights are drawing in,
It's getting darker earlier.

Frosty in the morning,
The grass is jewelled
And the fields are bare and brown.

Nuts fall off trees,
Leaves fall off trees,
When they fall they sway and swerve.

Emma Hughes (11)
Coed y Brain Primary School

THE MOON

The moon is a light bulb
hanging in the sky.

White paper flying in the
night sky.

A white ball kicked up
into space.

Jordan Gurner (8)
Coed y Brain Primary School

GOLD!

Gold is brightly shining, we both know
what it's like.
Gold is used for many things including
our teeth.
We wear it for fashion and for many
other things.
It's normally used for aeroplanes' windows
to keep the glare away.
It's wrapped around our fingers, it's
everywhere we look.
We use it for electric wires or connections
to watch TV.
It shines as bright as buttercups with a
bright, big gleam.
The quality can never end for we like
it very much.
Gold is as smooth as silk and as pretty
as a tulip.
When the sun shines on gold it is like a
ray of sun.
Gold is like the shimmering of the stars
and the moonlight.
Gold is like the sunshine.

Rhys Piper (11)
Coed y Brain Primary School

WINGS

If I had wings
I would visit the heavens.

If I had wings
I would eat a candyfloss cloud.

If I had wings
I would disappear with a rainbow.

If I had wings
I would walk the horses.

If I had wings
I would swim the volcanoes.

If I had wings
I would dive with the dolphins.

If I had wings
I would fly away into the blue full moon.

Kimberley Cooling (10)
Coed y Brain Primary School

THE PAUPER

The pauper is the colour of a dull brown.
He is the autumn season.
In a big, gloomy workhouse
On a wet, rainy day,
He is a dirty, ragged shirt
On a hard, wooden chair.
He is the sound of a wet wind
And the taste of mouldy bread.

Sarah Webber (10)
Coed y Brain Primary School

14

SOLAR SYSTEM

The sun the king of the ring.
Pluto the newborn king.
Jupiter the eldest prince.
Earth like a dog carrying fleas.
Mercury the number 1 racing car.
Jupiter with his red diamond.
Venus the thief of the heat.
The sun the king, Neptune the princess,
And all the others as the slaves.
Uranus the most slanted of the lot.
The sun like a gold ring.
Mars the chocolate bar.

Dale Owen (11)
Coed y Brain Primary School

AUTUMN

Autumn is here
Dew sparkles in the hazy sun.
Mist comes down like a thick blanket
The colourful leaves twirl like graceful dancers.
A rainbow of leaves spin from the bare trees
Tiny creatures scurry here and there to find safety for winter.
Ripe, juicy blackberries are waiting to be plucked.
Conkers fall from their spiky cases.
Birds migrate to Africa.
Summer has left us,
Autumn is truly here.

Vikee McTighe (11)
Coed y Brain Primary School

THE SOLAR SYSTEM

The sun, the queen high above
Tells her slaves to hurry up.
The slaves go round and round
To try and please this moody sun.
Jupiter says angrily:
'I have no energy.'
Gather around, gather around,
I shall give pure light,
Pluto hurry up, just stop lazing about,
Mars hurry up I want your orbit done,
All you planets weak and small
I want your deeds done great and small.

I am your sun,
Commander and queen of all
I expect you to treat me like your queen.

Emma Preece (10)
Coed y Brain Primary School

GOLD IS . . .

Gold is . . .
A nugget that was once buried treasure,
The long wavy hair of a princess in a fantasy,
The last golden apple hanging from a tree,
Golden leaves swaying in the wind,
Precious gold corn ready to be harvested,
The gold sand trickling through my toes,
A moonlit evening for two,
Golden eggs from a fairy tale,
And the petals of a flower.

Sophie Artus (10)
Coed y Brain Primary School

WINGS

If I had wings
I would slide down a rainbow
Into a cave full of gold.

If I had wings
I would sit on a cloud
And eat chocolate stars.

If I had wings
I would have a tea party in space
On Saturn's rings.

If I had wings
I would go to the Amazon
And ride on an alligator.

If I had wings
I would show Colin McRae
How to drive.

If I had wings
I would drive
Schumacher's Ferrari.

If I had wings
I would arrange the stars
To spell my name.

If I had wings
I would dive off the Eiffel Tower
Into France.

Simon Burnell (11)
Coed y Brain Primary School

AUTUMN

Have you seen the changing colours,
And the leaves falling off the trees?
It's getting darker, earlier every night,
As the nights get colder.

It is time for the final blaze of colour
As the morning gets its misty haze.
The grass is jewelled,
And the fields are bare and brown.

The nuts are falling off the trees
And so are the leaves,
In the nice warm breeze,
Changing colour.

Animals gather their winter store
As birds fly south, for the chilly winter ahead,
As the first of robins flutter,
What a season is autumn.

The evergreen trees keep their leaves,
As others go bare.
The harvest coming up in autumn,
The hunters moon shines gold.

Autumn is the loveliest season of all,
Everything happens to the animals,
As they start to get ready to hibernate,
It really is the best - *is autumn!*

Michael Gooding (11)
Coed y Brain Primary School

AUTUMN

It's autumn time again.
Soon there'll be dry, crisp leaves
drifting from the bare trees.
The shiny mahogany conkers break
away from their prickly cases
leaving their soft, prickly cases.

The weather is humid and wet.
Jack Frost is just around the corner
waiting to unleash his cold, frosty powers.
The squirrels collect nuts for
hibernation and the birds fly south.

Farmers reap the corn for harvest,
Blackberry tart is cut
letting out its delicious smell.

Matthew Tudball (11)
Coed y Brain Primary School

FIREWORK GLAZING

I can hear screeching, crackling and
bang!
Crash!
Bash!
Sizzling!
The smell of beefburgers sizzling,
A guy burning gently as one leg falls off.
On top of the bonfire lies a guy half burnt,
Bright colours shining like stars,
Hot fire blazing bright.

Abbie Parker (7)
Coed y Brain Primary School

BONFIRE NIGHT

Orange, purple, green, blue
firing out like a rainbow.

Going up in
the sky all
the smoke floating.

All the flames
blazing out
shooting the stars with their strength.

Their strength is
powerful just
like wind.

The wind blows
the fire - it explodes
just like gunpowder.

The crackle
is like people
shouting - children screaming
and babies crying.

Sarah Pugh (7)
Coed y Brain Primary School

THE MOON

The moon is a ball of glass
floating in the sky.

The moon is like a balloon
flying in the deep, dark air.

The moon's light reflects
on the deep, dark, calm sea.

The moon's light is like
a big, white diamond eyeball.

Lois Fitzpatrick (8)
Coed y Brain Primary School

RICH AND POOR

In sparkling cufflinks
I shall be dressed,
With golden cane.
I am impressed.

A tattered top
I have to wear,
A broken cane,
No one will care.

In a beautiful bonnet
I shall be dressed,
With silver parasol.
I am impressed.

A broken bonnet
I have to wear,
With battered parasol,
No one will care.

In silk and satin shirt
I shall be dressed,
With spats on my shoes.
I am impressed.

Daniel McTighe (10)
Coed y Brain Primary School

SIGHTS AND SOUNDS

My favourite sights are
A field full of colourful flowers,
Red, orange and mustard coloured leaves in the autumn,
Newborn ducklings waddling along,
Fireworks going off up into the sky and letting out
                                              lovely colours,
Babies walking for the first time,
Cold winter frost on the streets
And the beautiful sunset in the sky.

My favourite sounds are
Blackbirds singing to wake me up in the morning,
People cheering when their team wins a game,
The wind whistling past me on a windy day,
The sound of children playing,
Rain tapping on the roof at night,
Bubbling laughter coming from a tree house
And the sound of a rusty bell ringing in the playground.

Kayleigh O'Hanlon (11)
Coed y Brain Primary School

GOLD

Gold is as wonderful as the gleaming
stars in the night sky,
It is like a shining golden egg in a fairy tale,
Like a lion's mane sparkling in the sun,
It is like a sparkling moon in the dark blue sky,
As a golden apple hanging off a tree,
Like a crown waiting to be worn by a king,
It is a golden sand waiting for people to walk on it.

Hannah Pepperell (10)
Coed y Brain Primary School

GOLD IS . . .

Gold is a shimmering, golden rock,
A lion's magnificent golden mane,
The sparkling treasure inside the tomb of a great, golden pyramid
And a crown that shines like the melting sun.

It is the ripples of golden corn as the wind blows it,
The touch of Midas as whole buildings turned to gold,
A golden coin a metal detector has found,
The sand that stretches for miles and miles.

The precious sparkle of a mermaid's golden hair as she sits on a
                                                    rock combing it,
A star in space as it sparkles with an everlasting light,
The veins on a small rock out of the ground,
The golden heart of God.

Bruce Jenkins (11)
Coed y Brain Primary School

GOLD

Gold is the sparkling sun shining on the Earth,
It's the bright stars gleaming through the sky.
Gold is the bright sand by the seashore,
It's the nuggets that we dig for,
The corn getting ready for harvest.
Gold is the boiling hot fire burning its logs,
It's the precious ring that passes down the families,
It's the crown that belongs to the king sparkling as the sun
                                                    shines on him.

Racheal Kidley (10)
Coed y Brain Primary School

MY FIRST PENNY-FARTHING

My dad bought me a penny-farthing,
It had a wheel as big as me.
I just about got on it with the help of my dad.
I first wobbled, then fell off.
I grazed my knee and ruined my clothes.
My friends laughed and made fun,
But I did not care.
I just stepped on and rode through the streets.
It was like a dream come true,
Riding through the streets with
Everyone waving at me.
I felt great and cheerful.

Natalie Webber (10)
Coed y Brain Primary School

PYLONS

Pylons sitting in the field
Their muscular structure stands proud and true
The metal giants enormous and strong
They never lose their battles
They stand their ground all day
Shooting electricity from one place to another
They are the kings, the rulers of electricity.

Jonathan Mustafa (10)
Coed y Brain Primary School

A VICTORIAN CHILD WORKER

A Victorian child worker is the colour black.
He is the autumn season.
In a dusty, dark and dirty coal mine
On a dull, rainy day,
He is ripped, black trousers and a plain, white,
Tattered top.
He is a brown, dirty stool with one leg missing.
He is the sound of the cutting machine,
Cutting all the coal.
He is the taste of burnt toast.

Emma Littlewood (10)
Coed y Brain Primary School

WHAT CAN YOU DO WILD WINTER WIND?

I can
Rattle the windows till they shatter,
Make the night air freeze,
Make your hats blow off your head
And make you cold all through the night.
But I can't
Make your day peaceful
Or make your flowers grow.

David Bishop (9)
Coed y Brain Primary School

THE MOON

The moon is like a frosty, cold face
floating across the sky.

The moon is like a very cold, dark
and light place.

The moon reminds me of the times when
I was young and my mother saying
that the moon is Jimmy moon.

Its reflection on the sea looks like a
path up to the moon.

Katie Hewer (7)
Coed y Brain Primary School

THE WORKHOUSE

The old, old workhouse
Stood alone.
Fix us, fix us,
Mend the rusty pipes,
Repair the rotting floorboards,
Put the bricks back on the wall,
Put the window back into place,
Paint the door bright and colourful,
Clean the dirty and dusty floor,
And put everything like it used to be.

Kylie Fox (10)
Coed y Brain Primary School

EARTHQUAKE

I sat down on my sofa,
Mum ironed my shirt,
Then I felt a tremor,
It seemed to shake the earth!

My mum fell over,
The iron hit my old kite,
The TV set exploded,
The room was now alight!

Windows shattered
And ornaments fell,
Trapped in an inferno,
I thought I was in hell!

Mum slowly got to her feet,
I dived to the door,
But before I got there,
A hole shattered the floor!

I tumbled to the apartment below,
The whole neighbourhood was on fire,
'Everything will be okay!' screamed Mum,
I knew she was a liar.

I slowly rose,
My ankle was shattered.
Mum helped me up,
Out of the window I saw bodies scattered.

I suppose that I was lucky,
To fortunately survive,
That terrible earthquake,
Richter scale mark five.

Chris Williams (11)
Coed y Brain Primary School

I Am An Evacuee

Thinking of family,
Holding tight to bag,
Waving to my mum.
Carrying my gas mask,
Crying and hugging my mum.
Food in a box,
Feeling very worried,
Label on my clothes.

Megan Black (9)
Coed y Brain Primary School

The Fish

The swimming fish, swimming all day,
In the sea
And in the bowl.

The swimming fish, swimming all day,
Having fun swimming around,
In my room
With me to play with,
In the day and in the night.

The swimming fish, swimming all day
With her friend,
The golden fish.
They swim together all day.

My fish are the best.

Sophie Halliday (9)
Craig-y-Nos School

FLOWERS

Red, yellow, pink, green and blue,
The colours of a rainbow they are too.
Yellow are daffodils, red are roses,
They are white and pink too.
Don't forget the forget-me-nots, they are blue.
As well as daffodils, buttercups are yellow too.

Lotte Williams (9)
Craig-y-Nos School

THE ARMY TANK

The army tank
has bombs, cogs, machine guns and bullets.
They have computers in the tanks.
Soldiers go in the tanks.
Bravely they go over the bridges.
To fight the enemy!

Lewis James Upton (8)
Craig-y-Nos School

MY LOVELY FOOTBALL

I adore football
It's my favourite subject
I don't understand why!
When you score you dance around
And everybody jumps on you.
I like football I shout *Goal!*
And everybody cheers.

Thomas James Maimone (8)
Craig-y-Nos School

CHRISTOPHER CAT

Christopher cat, Christopher cat,
Christopher's sitting on the door mat.
Christopher purrs this song all day long
He doesn't even care when the clock goes bong.
Bong, bong, bong,
Bong, bong, bong.
Six o'clock and he still won't stop
And all his owners want to go to the shop.
But they can't go because Christopher cat
Is sitting on the door mat.

Kirsty Shepherd (9)
Craig-y-Nos School

WHILST WALKING IN THE WOODS

Whilst walking in the woods one day
I came across an animal
I didn't move, I didn't speak
Yet there it was!
It had the face of a skunk
A body of a tiger
The tail of a lion
It looked so fierce.
But soon I ran from it
It saw me in the bushes
So I ran and ran and ran.

Christopher Thomas (9)
Craig-y-Nos School

SCHOOL

People say you get an education at school.
Mathematics, English, science and history
These are some of the subjects at school.
Picking books from a library to read for school.

Friday: is homework day
This week we are finding out words
like queries for school.
Monday: swimming front crawl and butterfly
back to school we go in the mini bus.
Wednesday: yeepy gym day forward and backward
rolls, cart-wheels and hand stands at school.
Friday: tennis day - forehands and backhands at school.
End of the week - what a week!
I think it's time to say goodnight.

Amy Freya Collings (7)
Craig-y-Nos School

MY DAD AND I

My dad and I are so close together
that nothing can come between us.
My dad and I spend the most time together.
That's when Dad's not away!
I love my dad - he's great.

Mind you! When Mum's around
he pretends to be rather strict, but
actually . . .
He's the best dad in the world!

Lysette Emma Owen (8)
Craig-y-Nos School

SCHOOL

Whenever I go to school
I think and say what will I do
First of all I say *Hi!*
To my wonderful teacher Mrs Fursland
If I am lucky I just see Mrs Davies,
but sometimes Lysette comes and says
'Got your music with you today?'
Every sunny day whenever
Mrs Fursland opens the window.
I get a little breeze
and it brightens up my day.

Lydia Sarah-Grace Isherwood (8)
Craig-y-Nos School

MY BEAUTIFUL HOUSE

I have a messy house
but I love it so much
I have a garden with lots of plants - all different kinds.
I have nice comfy chairs
and a sofa.
I have a huge bed and it's
nice and cosy.
I wouldn't like to live somewhere else.

Neal Shepherd (7)
Craig-y-Nos School

NEW YORK

New York is full of buildings
Full of flash cars
Full of corny people
Full of movie stars
Everyone is rich. Dollars! Dollars!
That's all they have.
Oh look! There's George Clooney
I've got to get his autograph.
This is the best place I've been to in my life!

Kristian Limpert (7)
Craig-y-Nos School

SAFARI

Hippos charging like mad bulls,
And crocodiles drowning
Like fish being hooked by fear.
Swinging monkeys
All over the trees like branches,
Falling down and down to other sights.

Storming cheetahs all over the place,
Like fast animals going down hills,
And jumping like rabbits
In and out of their burrows.

Scratching lions,
Slithery snakes going to other
Positions every time.

Lee Sinclair (9)
Cwmllynfell Primary School

WORMS

Little worms so disgusting and waterlogged,
Living in their world of rotting vegetation,
Smelling so foul.
People staying away from the compost heap.

Enemies flying so powerfully,
Eating their prey so joyfully.
Then gliding to nests to feed their young,
And sleep.

Pink little worms so microscopic,
Moving is their hobby.
Sliding to the left, right, up and down,
That's all they can complete.

Now it's sunset . . .
That's night for the living things
That shut their tiny eyes.
The sun goes down,
The moon rises,
This wriggling creature waits for sunrise.

Zeke Davies (10)
Cwmllynfell Primary School

MORNINGS

It starts in the night,
How do the colours get so bright?
Dawn awakes
The mysterious world.

Spark of sunshine
Glimpse of light
Morning is here
So colourful and bright.

Cerys Davies (10)
Cwmllynfell Primary School

A SNOWY DAY

One patterned snowflake,
Then comes another,
        The ground is full.
How amazing, one more hour to go.
        So beautiful
        So white
Like a star shining bright.
Some children have no school,
        So lucky . . .

Children dancing in the snow,
        Some sliding
        Some rolling
        What a sight!
Suddenly the snow stops.
Children laughing
Around the land
Wolves howling
Snow is here once again.

Llinos Catrin Flowers (11)
Cwmllynfell Primary School

BIRTHDAYS

Waking up in the morning
Full of excitement.
Rushing down stairs like a cheetah.
Oh the happiness . . .
The presents
Cards
And the love and care.

Oh, I love it when it's my birthday.
I like it because I get
Presents
Cards
Love
Care
A party
A birthday cake
And loads of other things.

Kirsty Leanne Griffiths (9)
Cwmllynfell Primary School

DOGS

I wake up in the morning,
Dogs barking, dogs scratching
Each other.

Walking and running,
Owners say stop!
Shouting loudly at the dogs.

At night the dogs are sleeping,
Calm and warm.

Kirsty Louise Thomas (10)
Cwmllynfell Primary School

FORMULA 1

Formula 1 cars buzzing on the track,
Like bees flying with their sacks of nectar.
Damon Hill, the black and yellow Jordan,
Michael Schumacher, the red Ferrari,
David Coulthard, the black and grey MacLaren,
Champions of the world . . .
Fast pits working all day.
Swapping tyres, wet or dry.
Cars crashing all the way,
Need a pit stop right away.

Burning cars, picked up by cranes,
Firemen say 'Get out of the way!'
End of the race for cars that don't work,
Other cars struggling for first.

The finishing line is two miles away,
Crowds whistling like the wind.
Racers going faster and faster,
Burning their own rubber.

At last, the finishing line.
This a challenge for all the heroes.
Cars like bullets shooting past the flag.
Up on the stand British fans screaming,
Damon Hill has won the race!

Back at the club a big party,
All the drivers are happy.
Damon Hill celebrating his win.
Colourful cars resting in the shed.
What a good sport!

Rhodri Allcock (9)
Cwmllynfell Primary School

BADGERS

Fierce badgers all over the place,
Working like miners,
Digging their holes
And getting muddy
As they work their shifts
Throughout the day.

The sun awakens,
And opens its eyes.
Badgers get up
All heads pop out.
A black and brown creature comes forth,
Its walk is so stylish.

His helmet is on, ready for work,
The work today is catching its prey.
Catching it like a bear
Taking it back to its lair.

The sun goes down, the moon wakes up.
Those thousands of eyes, like fireflies.
I never knew a badger's life could be such strife!

Gareth Harries (9)
Cwmllynfell Primary School

VOICES OF THE PEOPLE

Voices of people all around
Some are happy, maybe grumpy.
Babies screaming, cars revving,
Adults shouting at their kids!

Some laughing, some crazy,
For no sleep in the night.
Her Majesty comes,
Peace and quiet at last.

Rhodri Evans (10)
Cwmllynfell Primary School

MOUNTAINS

Mountains with lots of animals,
Sheep, horses of all kinds.
Grass so green, new and fresh,
Hikers, walkers climbing up steep hills.

Up the mountain, dark and early
Owls and sheep that give you the creeps,
I like the mountain in the light.
Trees swaying, rabbits playing and eating,
It's so beautiful.

Rocks all over the mountain
Where old quarries have been.
Dumped cars, burnt and useless
Look like rusted metal frames.

Grass dancing in the wind
Blowing in the night
When it's pitch black.
The place is deserted.

Steffan Rees (10)
Cwmllynfell Primary School

MILLENNIUM

Exciting and miraculous millennium
A new century, a new year!
Outstanding tune so cheerful and loud
Fantastic night of celebration!

Having fun
Jumping around
Anxiously waiting
For that clock to strike 12.

One more hour
Millennium is here!
Thrilling and restless
Throughout the world.
People like horses
Running around
No one can wait
For that hour to sound.

Charlotte Austin (10)
Cwmllynfell Primary School

FLOWERS

Roses, bluebells, poppies
light, bright, incredible!
Daisies, buttercups and daffodils,
See them bloom in the beautiful sun.
A blue sheet has covered the sky,
How nice, how delightful!

The rain starts with one, two, three,
Baby flowers just starting to grow.
Little daisies around your neck.
How did God create such beauties.

Catrin Richards (9)
Cwmllynfell Primary School

THE SUN

The sun is the biggest star
It's full of flames and gas
Gives sunlight in all kinds of ways.

This star, so bright and glittery,
Not round at all, but circular.
Bright, bright yellow it rises
And in the night it falls.

Rain and sun make a lovely rainbow,
I like the sun, it keeps us nice and warm.
It can help grow things like
Plants and vegetables,
And many, many more.

Now you know all about the sun
There's nothing more to hear.
So just have an excellent life
With the sun.

Abby Lynne Davies (9)
Cwmllynfell Primary School

FROGS

Slimy and wet creatures
Camouflaged on leaves,
Soft and delicate
As delicate as fleas.

Jumpy and awkward
Swimming all day,
Like professionals
Among their prey.

Lumpy and wet
Horrible and disgusting,
Say the people.

Jumping up and down
That's all they can do.
Good night say all the little ones
We love you.

Nicholas Wyn Stephens (10)
Cwmllynfell Primary School

CUTE CATS

Cute cats, big and strong,
Unfortunate whiskers big and long.
Tame, but mouse catchers!
Everybody needs these pets.

Cuddly and fluffy creatures,
Active, good hunters.
Tame, fussy and fast,
Some I hope, will last.
I love cute cats.

Helen Jones (10)
Cwmllynfell Primary School

HORSES

Horses running, dancing, prancing
Stallions calling mares
Horses eating, crunching, munching
Some sleeping, some snoring.

Black and white colts
Colourful fillies
Handsome geldings
Dull foals.

Colts bucking
Foals biting
Mares rearing
Geldings have colic.

Katy Thomas (11)
Cwmllynfell Primary School

FIRE

Fire yellow as a chick
Red as someone's blood
As tall as a building
As wide as a car
Bright as the sun
As scary as a ghost.
Looks like a daffodil with a red middle.
Sounds like crackling fireworks.
Tastes like my tongue is on fire
Smells like smoke floating.

Steven Arthur Gibbons (9)
Groes Primary School

FIRE

Scarlet flames shot up like trees
as his fumes choke you.
He lets out a cackle
His scarlet face
With eyes like a demon
and a voice like a lion.
Spitting and hissing with breath
as hot as a dragons.
Rising up a deep crimson
Power increasing
Then dying down
Like the setting sun
Soon burnt out,
Leaving only ebony ashes behind.

Anna Bowyer (10)
Groes Primary School

THE SEA

Dawn shows
The sea tastes saltier than ever
A fish tank in the middle of nowhere
Suddenly there's a twist - sucking things down!
The sea crashed against the rocks
Sea - wet as if people are crying.
The foam like a warm bath.
The aqua wave ripples
The everlasting rolling sea!

Roisin Nicola Mollaghan (10)
Groes Primary School

UNDERGROUND

Under the ground in a deep, dull hole
The hunter lives.
He wanders down the dark, lonely
tunnel . . . searching.
A stench wafts up his nose.
A sound like no other.
It went silent
Not a sound to hear.
Walking through the soggy mud.
Creeping slowly.
The damp walls glistening.
The horrid noise was heard again.
He stopped sharply!
A bat flew past, it blew his hair.
He thought he saw the end
Round the bend, turns as quick
as a flash.
Out of sight!

Karley Louise Jack (10)
Groes Primary School

FOREST POEMS

I walk in - the trees loom over like giant's hands
All dark and lonely
Silence, darkness approaches.
The grass is soft like cottonwool.
The trees are angry
The sky is ebony
The storm approaches . . .
But the forest is calm and happy.

Alexya Lois Davies (10)
Groes Primary School

THE SEA

The lonely waves shimmer in the sunlight.
A complete silence
Runs throughout its waters
Before the storm came.
Roaring beasts whine for attention,
As the ugly shadow grows nearer.
Deep waters like an abyss
Ripples with fear
As if they're being pierced with a thousand spears.
All colours slowly die
Being captured by the deadly mist.
But soon the horizon lifts,
Quieting the warriors of the mighty sea.

Katherine Haylock (10)
Groes Primary School

FIRE

Red hot like an oven
Blistering as it goes on
Like an orange with flames
Extending into the ebony sky.

As angry as the storm
It wants to kill.
A horrible stench
With a choking taste.
Until it dies away.

Mathew John Needs (10)
Groes Primary School

THE SEA

Dawn arrives
The aqua waves begin to ripple
Children dipping their toes into
the cool foam.
A twisting starts
Water whooshes around
Sucking children into the salty abyss.
Taking their last breath
Coughing
Spluttering
This gigantic monster is
hungry for more.

Jane Anne Ahearne (10)
Groes Primary School

THE SEA

Walking down the dusty road going to the sea
As the waves crash up to splash you.
You can taste the horrible taste of sea salt.
Stuck down your chest.
Picking up your feet over crumbly sand.
The pebbles are rocky and hard.
The big yellow sun moving away
Bringing in the horrible rain.
Please don't bring in the disgusting.
Horrible evening roar.

Natalie Jones (10)
Groes Primary School

UNDERGROUND

Robots dominate rock-hard ground
People scuttling underground
like ants to their nest.
A cramped, gloomy tunnel.
People crying 'There is no hope!'
The burning air making people faint.

But . . .
They had an idea
A ship
As huge as a tree
As long as a mile.
Hopes rise for human-kind.

But . . .
The gigantic bang
The ship sinks
A world turns into Armageddon.
Will mankind survive?

Thomas Ronan (9)
Groes Primary School

YELLOW

Lemon yellow colour
A happy gentle colour
Full of grace and warmth
It's bright and gay
Not cold or plain.
The sun in space burning around the world.
Daffodils swaying in the wind.
Chicks cheeping away.

Ian Billington (10)
Groes Primary School

FOREST

Sunshine peaking through the enormous trees
Smelling like an open water melon.
Tasting like fresh air.
Sounding like a harp playing in the distance.
Thousands of leaves perching above
Wild life hopping, jumping around.
A black tunnel in front of us.
As we get near the air gets dirtier,
Walking towards it like a widow crossing the road.
Scatter, the forest crumbles to the ground.

Matthew Saker (10)
Groes Primary School

THE FOREST

In the dark and gloomy forest
Trees loomed like witches fingers.
Trees swayed in the breeze
Leaves rustled like cockroaches
scuttling across the floor.
Daylight got gloomy
Fog lowered
All became silent
Not a movement or a sound
could be heard.

Richard William Griffiths (9)
Groes Primary School

FIRE POEM

Fire - red, hot as hell below
as angry as the devil himself.
Raging his smoky scent
that blacks out rooms, and sends people
to their death.
He crackles in your throat like popping candy
and smells like coal burning in a fireplace.
His body, as bright as a robin's red chest.
He burns his flames, like elephants
reaching out their trunks.
And acts like a bully in a school playground.
But water gets thrown
and he soon dies down,
leaving nothing but ashes and smoke.

Nia Jayne Bamsey (9)
Groes Primary School

FIRE

The fire was sparkling like stars in the sky
Flaming bright as if it was angry.
Burning like a comet from space
Hot like the sun
Scorching
You could almost taste the smoke.
The fire blistering
Then quiet . . .
Like a little mouse.

Shamal Miah (9)
Groes Primary School

UNDERGROUND

Dripping pipes and cars above me
was what I could hear.
Terrified, looking around,
something caught my eye.
Something crept across the gory stones
I was scared, very scared.
A horrifying sound . . .
Slam!
I ran fast
Wind blowing through my hair
I came to a halt.
I was stuck
I came to a place with
slimy walls and rocks falling.
Hands stretched out like branches of trees.
pulled me out,
A stench
Feeling wet
A fall . . .
He was out of sight!

Courtney Pugh (10)
Groes Primary School

MILLLENNIUM

Year 2000 will be the best time of my life,
Fireworks going.
The computers are bugging
Everyone having a good time
This is the day when everyone wonders
What's going to happen?

Leigh Price (10)
Gwaunfarren Primary School

THE MILLENNIUM

It will soon be the new millennium.
Will all the computers crash?
They have been programmed
till the end of 1999.
So what will happen after that?
Will our videos work?
When we wake up on the 1st of January
2000 will we have any electricity?
Will the Millennium Dome be finished in time?
What will happen in the next century?
Only time will tell!

Stephen Thomas (11)
Gwaunfarren Primary School

CELEBRATION 2000

The year 2000
I can't wait
To see the clock hands strike twelve,
I'll be standing at the gate.
The Millennium Bug
Is the worry to be,
To see if they find a cure for it,
We'll all wait and see!
The year 2000
How will it be?
Well, how will it be?
That'll be the year I'd like to see.

Rhydian Gareth Patterson (11)
Gwaunfarren Primary School

CELEBRATION 2000

I'm rather worried and I'll go berserk,
if my brand new PC refuses to work.
Today in Asda nobody was jolly,
as they crashed and banged and filled
up their trolley.

They fought over bread and wrestled over meat,
and pints of milk smashed at their feet.
When we got home we felt very hearty,
as we cooked all the food and changed for the party.

Once in a lifetime out in the street,
friends and loved ones have
come to meet.
To share in the pleasure, the joy and the fun,
Goodbye to the old year - the millennium has come.

Uncle Sid got up and told a little jokey,
while my Auntie Mary was stuck to the microphone
on the karaoke.
They laughed and they sang and the street was alight,
the spectrum of fireworks lit up the night.
The clock struck 12 and the fun had just begun,
I won't see the millennium again . . .
But I can't wait for 2001!

Bethan Jones (10)
Gwaunfarren Primary School

CELEBRATION 2000!

It's the 2nd millennium,
To the New Year shall we
survive,
From Millie the bug.
Us computers are afraid,
Please shut us down,
Until the bug has gone.
Don't throw us away,
you will regret it.
We computers don't want to
malfunction.
Please, please, shut us down!

Lee Greenaway (11)
Gwaunfarren Primary School

CELEBRATION 2000

In the year 2000 computers will crash
And it will be the start of a new century.
There will be parties all around the world.
There will be thousands of people around Big Ben
Waiting for his bell to signal midnight.
When it rings that will signal the brand new century.
On the stroke of midnight everyone will sing
Auld Lang Syne.
And will look forward to what the new century
will bring.

Jonathan Thomas (11)
Gwaunfarren Primary School

CELEBRATION 2000

The year 2000 is a special event,
lots of things will happen.
The Sydney Olympic Games will be held
and Wales will win with the baton.
In the year 2000 we will
probably have lots of new inventions.
We might have different types of clothes
and different types of fashions.
Will we have telephones, where we
can see who we talk to?
Or will we have different types of
sports with footballs or rugby balls?
Will the computers understand the
date 2000?
Or will they just crash!
We will have to see when
the year 2000 comes.

Hana Imiolczyk (10)
Gwaunfarren Primary School

CELEBRATION 2000

In the year 2000, people all over the world,
will celebrate the new century.
I wonder if things will change, I wonder if they'll stay the same?
The millennium stadium is being built,
fireworks are going
computers are bugging.
This is the day when everybody wonders what's going to happen!

Keith Phillips (11)
Gwaunfarren Primary School

MILLENNIUM 2000

Mummy goes shopping, daddy goes for a drink.
Better hurry up before the party begins.
In the house, we party all night long.
Listening to the music in a rapping song.
Let's lower the music before the bells ring.
Everybody knows the New Year is about to begin
Now let's get our glass to cheer the New Year.
Now that everyone is here.
In the town there's silence but not for long
United together we will all be for the New Year
Millennium.

Marie Louise Morgans (10)
Gwaunfarren Primary School

THE YEAR 2000

Party in the year 2000!
Next year there are going to be
Big parties because it
Is the millennium.
People are going to celebrate
So people will be having parties
On their street.
People will be hiring
Places for the millennium
So the people can
Buy tickets for the party of
A lifetime!

Tara Jones (10)
Gwaunfarren Primary School

CELEBRATION 2000

The people countdown from ten to one
With anticipation of things to come.
Happy New Year, it's the millennium.
Celebrations around the globe,
People flocking to visit the Dome.
Travelling to far-off places
Lots of happy smiling faces.
To see the dawn of the new millennium.

Everyone giving each other a hug
Computers compatible, no Millennium Bug!
Festivities planned well in advance
It's party time! Let's all dance,
And wish each other all the best,
'Hip, hip, hooray' you'll hear them say
'Three cheers for the millennium!'

Lois Dale Jenkins (11)
Gwaunfarren Primary School

MILLENNIUM

Here comes the millennium!
I won't see another one.
There will be a Millennium Bug,
which will cause chaos around.
Computers will crash,
but don't throw them in the trash.
Just shut them down.
Don't have a frown.

Daniel Foley (10)
Gwaunfarren Primary School

MILLENNIUM

I wonder what the millennium will be like!
Will it be different, or the same?
Will I be the inventor of a brand new game?
No one knows!

Will we drive on the road, or in the air?
Will we go on holidays to the moon, Jupiter - anywhere?
No one knows!

Hologram trees and purple grass,
Invisible mirrors for a looking glass.
Rocket houses, floating chairs,
Ferocious kittens and gentle bears.
No one knows!

Starving people a thing of the past,
No more wars, peace at last.
No more drugs or Millennium Bugs,
Stop the global warming or you're real thugs.

Christian Evans (10)
Gwaunfarren Primary School

THE MILLENNIUM BUG

Will the computers understand 1/1/00
or will they all just crash?
Will the computers go all to pot or
become worthless like trash?
Will the computers go down the drain
and lose all types of information.
Or scarier still, what will happen if this
bug takes over the nation!

Craig Rhys Barlow (11)
Gwaunfarren Primary School

CELEBRATING THE YEAR 2000

Year 2000 everybody sings,
Let's have a party and sing, sing, sing.
Year 2000 will be a funny thing,
Major trouble is coming.
Computers are great,
Computers are fun,
Will they work in the year 2000.
Will it change the world,
Or will it stay the same?

Everyone stocking food,
For who knows what just might happen.
People see the millennium,
People watch it on TV.
It's still the same,
But will everything stay the same
Or will everything change?
Time will tell!

People all over the world will celebrate
As twelve o'clock arrives.
The bells will ring
The bells will chime
As everybody sings
People wonder what the future will bring.

Sarah Ford (10)
Gwaunfarren Primary School

MILLENNIUM

Computer crash at twelve one night
The computer your pride and joy, delight.
TV's, fridges, lights and all
At that moment . . . millennium calls
Until the mechanics can sort it out,
Just sit in the corner and sulk and pout!

James Cushen (10)
Gwaunfarren Primary School

MILLENNIUM

The year 2000 is coming
All the parties are going to be numbing
Come to these parties, it's your last chance
We will all be getting ready
All getting ready for the big party
In the parties which are coming,
With the music we will be humming
This will be the millennium!

Hannah Stokes (8)
Hendre Junior School

WHAT WILL HAPPEN?

In the new millennium, will we have cars?
Will we have phones?
Will we go to a distant planet?
So what will we do?
Will there be life on the earth?
Who knows what will happen?
In the new millennium.

Jonathan Rees (8)
Hendre Junior School

CELEBRATION 2000

C alling, singing up the street, lots of these type of people you
will meet
E nding the millennium is a happy day, people shouting, hip hip
hooray! (for old people of course)
L ots of parties for everyone, get an invite so you can come
E ating, drinking and being merry, on your cocktail comes a cherry
B ooming fireworks in the air, there goes the roller-coaster in the fair
R anting, raving you won't hear - wow wee it's a new year
A lways and forever will the millennium stay in my heart,
never am I going to trade it for a cookie or a tart
T ry as you might, everyone will party all night
I ndia, Britain, USA all are celebrating, whey hey
O ver one billion will celebrate when 2000 is the date
N ot celebrating? Are you sad or have committed a crime and
that's bad?

Jamie Jackson (9)
Hendre Junior School

CELEBRATION 2000

C elebrations are fun for everyone
E veryone stays up late
L ovely parties we have all night
E veryone will enjoy themselves
B ad boys and girls will not get any presents
R ather have a big cake
A fter the party we go to bed
T ones of colour on the wall
I enjoy parties
O n their holidays they celebrate
N o one celebrates today, anyway.

Rachel McCarthy (9)
Hendre Junior School

THE NEW MILLENNIUM

In the new millennium our journey
will be faster up to the stars.

In the new millennium I hope my
Nintendo survives.

In the new millennium I want to be a boxer.
In the new millennium will there be cars?
In the new millennium I hope the shops are the same.

In the new millennium in London
they'll have a new Dome.

In the new millennium there's going to be
lots of parties.

In the new millennium there's going to be
lots of songs.

Ryan David Forehead
Hendre Junior School

MILLENNIUM

M is for music we hear all around
I is for invitation to a party with sound
L is for lights from the fireworks at night
L is for love and the meaning of life
E is for echoes of people, who shout
N is for neighbours who all come out
N is for news of this special time
I is for interesting tales - yours and mine
U is for Universe and all of the world
M is for millennium the celebration of the year!

Bechan Carpenter (8)
Hendre Junior School

SPORT

Player of Liverpool
Score and score
Go to France for a football tour
Win the Premiership
Get the Cup
Years to come you'll have good luck.

Try being a star, it's very hard
You get on the pitch and feel like lard
It's really depressing when you hit the post
You play in Brazil and really roast.

It's really scary when you play Benfica
After the match you have chicken tikka
After the meal you feel really sick
You hear the clock going tick, tick, tick.

You get drunk with a glass of beer
You wake up with an end to your career.

Richard Kestell (10)
Hendre Junior School

THINGS HAPPENING IN THE NEW MILLENNIUM

Funny parties happening
Fizzy drinks fizzing
Wild clowns dancing
Happy people shouting
Long streamers sleeping
Bouncy balloons bursting
All in the new millennium.

Rachel Davies (8)
Hendre Junior School

MILLENNIUM RECIPE

Go shopping for some food and drink
Invite some friends
Have a disco or a concert
Play some games
Eat lots of sweets and chocolate
Have lots of fun with party poppers
Play with lots of balloons and dance to some music
Make lots of pancakes or jump into the air
Have lots of surprises in the millennium
All the computers will go off and don't be sad, be glad.
When the clock strikes twelve the fireworks go off.
Have a nice night in the millennium.

Verity Davies (8)
Hendre Junior School

SPECIAL MILLENNIUM

M is for the new millennium
I   is for imagining jazz bands and celebrations
L is for the bright light at night
L is for the light at night which is bright
E is for the excitement in the night
N is for the special nights
N is for night and with the bright light at night
I   is for invitations to parties and discos
U is for umbrella when it rains
M is for mummy, making cakes, mmm mmm.

Jenna Swan (7)
Hendre Junior School

MILLENNIUM

Celebration in the crowds
Celebration in the clouds
Celebration in the shops
from the lovely smell
of hippie hops.

Celebration by water splashing
madly for the day.
Minutes, hours, go past like little
stones lashing by.
Nothing more to say goodbye
but the day is over
so - goodnight!

Laura McKinty (8)
Hendre Junior School

MILLENNIUM

C elebrate the year two thousand
E veryone laughs at the New Year
L isten to the party begin
E very person likes the gifts
B anging noises are all around
R inging bells stop the people so they can make a speech
A nd I watch the people dance all night
T hey have a street party and they eat burgers
I wave bye bye as the party ends
O n the stairs I fall asleep
N o one is home . . . it's all so quiet.

Bethan Newbury (9)
Hendre Junior School

MILLENNIUM

M is for a magnificent new century
I is for the interesting new dome in London
L is for loud music and parties in the streets
L is for learning new things about the millennium
E is for everybody who celebrates on New Years Day
N is for new foods and drinks that are made in the millennium
N is for new exciting things made in the millennium
I is for the interesting song called Millennium
U is for unemployed people who will probably find new jobs
M is for the millennium bug that will attack computers.

Stacey Spargo (9)
Hendre Junior School

MILLENNIUM

M usic and games have started
I nvitations are in all the shops
L ights are flashing on and off
L ots of balloons and lots of fun
E xcitement going around
N ice things will happen tonight
N ew millennium coming
I t's the year 2000.
U nited, the world will celebrate.
M illennium, a new one has begun.

Kadie Louise Ruck (8)
Hendre Junior School

2000, 2000

Quick let's have a party at my house,
don't cry there's not one mouse!
We'll dance and sing, oh dear me who comes in!
Oh no, it's my mum, don't worry let's still have fun!

In comes mum with a shock,
'Please dear will you go down the shop?'
I come down from the shop and *celebrate!*
Mum shouted but all the windows cracked because dad sang like a rat!

Oh no, half past nine, time for bed,
but on the way I bumped my head.
In the morning in comes my dad,
I was out cold but it was the best night
I ever had!

Danielle Wood (9)
Hendre Junior School

MILLENNIUM

M illennium separates 1000 years apart
I   listen to the music playing in my heart
L   isten to all the people shout all day
L   oads of food, we are so full
E   ating, dancing all day long
N   itter natter, nitter natter all the time
N   atter nitter, natter nitter, I'll have a headache when the clocks chime
I   'll be ill in the morning and the doctor will give me a warning
U   ncle Fred will be in bed with a serious hangover
M illennium is once again over and no more music in the heart.

Gemma Morgan & Lindsey Jones (10)
Hendre Junior School

MILLENNIUM BUG

Millennium Bug, Millennium Bug,
go back to where you came from.
Millennium Bug, Millennium Bug,
nobody likes you round here.
Millennium Bug, Millennium Bug,
most of us will have our computers off.
If it's broad daylight, evening or night you'll never get us.

Dane Hutton (9)
Hendre Junior School

MILLENNIUM 2000

Millennium is a new year
You wait and wait until the year 2000
You party, party all night
You watch the clock going tick tock, tick tock
Twelve comes, shake a hand
You eat and drink, eat and drink
Then you go to bed for forty winks!

Charlotte Harper (9)
Hendre Junior School

MILLENNIUM HITS THE HOUSE

The millennium starts when the clock strikes twelve.
People dancing, people singing, children shouting.
Millennium, millennium, ringing in my ears.
Party poppers go bang, bang, bang.
Dad's got drunk in the pub.
Mum's gone crazy, I think she's drunk!
Party over, it's another day.

Rebecca Mannings (9)
Hendre Junior School

THE MILLENNIUM SUPER MATCH

Players of Man U
Win the Cup
Go to Liverpool and get good luck
You run on the pitch
You score a goal
You get fouled later
And you rumble like coal
You walk down the tunnel, after the match
You sit on the bench
And say oh what a match
You have some water
When you walk out of the grounds
And you hear the crowd making funny sounds.

Daniel Jones (9)
Hendre Junior School

MILLENNIUM CELEBRATION

M illennium celebration.
I t is a time of happiness,
L et us all celebrate.
L et's all be happy!
E veryone celebrates,
N ew Year is here,
N ew century is here.
I t is a time of celebration.
U ntil it is over.
M illennium is a time of happiness.

Blaine Harrington (9)
Hendre Junior School

MILLENNIUM, WHEN THE CLOCK STRIKES TWELVE

When the clock strikes twelve the millennium begins
And Big Ben's bell rings out.

The wine comes out
Party poppers come out and go bang.

People scream and shout about the house . . .
Millennium.

We all go home and go to bed to rest our heads.

Laura Davies (10)
Hendre Junior School

PARTIES FOR MILLENNIUM

We have parties with loads of food
Some are boring, some are good
We invite all our friends
Some of the parties never, never end . . .

Bring some money, buy a drink then look at the time
It makes you think it's time for bed!
We all rush home and find . . .
We're all alone.

Arianna Willetts (10)
Hendre Junior School

MILLENNIUM, MILLENNIUM

Today is a start of a new year
Having a party up in the air
Here comes the Catherine wheel spinning around
Followed by a rocket shot from the ground

It's time for the countdown
All the people gather around counting down
10 . . . 9 . . . 8 . . . 7 . . . 6 . . . 5 . . . 4 . . . 3 . . . 2 . . . 1 . . .

Then from the crowd shouting out loud
Millennium, millennium is here
Yes, a new start of a new year!

Sarah Giurani (10)
Hendre Junior School

AEROPLANE

Metal bird flying above
Like a golden eagle or a dove

Going on holiday in your care
Flying and flying in mid-air

I get to the airport, say goodbye
I will really miss you, I don't lie

I really don't mind, I'm not going to stay
I can go on again another day!

Christopher Hutchings (10)
Hendre Junior School

MILLENNIUM 2000

When the clock gets to twelve
Hats go up, party poppers go off.

People scream, people shout
Bring the new year in and take the old one out.

Some then might go to bed and rest their heads.
Why not? The night is now dead!

Laura Jenkins (9)
Hendre Junior School

DISH-WASHING BRUSH

Red
as a rose
White
like snow
Silk
like a soft thread
Bumpy
like a road
Crushy
like a biscuit
Solid
like a cube
Spiky
like a bramble bush
Material
like a skirt.

Melissa Brown (9)
Jenner Park Primary School

A WOOD

I feel intimidated, petrified.
My hands shaking like an earthquake.
I can hear twigs snapping like the breaking of fingers.
Sinister footsteps leading their way
Across the antiquated nature trail.
I feel like a poor and helpless rabbit
Cornered by a pack of artful wolves,
Persecuting me.
The formidable lightning alarms me
Like the snap of a crocodile's jaw.
The trees look as if they want to reach out
Their bony, mossy fingers and . . .
Capture me.

Thomas Davie (10)
Jenner Park Primary School

A STREET

I felt scared,
tried to scream,
just so scared,
wolves howling in the distance
like the wind.
All covered in very thick mist,
I try to scream,
nothing came out.
The old scraps of newspaper floating
like a paraglider in the sky.

Nicholas James (10)
Jenner Park Primary School

WATER LILY RIVER

The shadows of the water lily river
Twisting and turning like never before.
Bending leaves, spiky bushes,
Bright shining blossoms
Swaying down the river
Like the current of the Atlantic Ocean.
It feels like I've found a beautiful deserted island.
The water as clear as crystal
Like the Caribbean lakes.
The long dark roots of small trees
Plunging into the water
Like swans gliding into the sea,
Tranquil,
Motionless,
Not a single noise around . . .
Paradise.

Michael Jenkins (11)
Jenner Park Primary School

THE ENCOUNTER

Crackle, sparkle goes the fire,
The dwarfs staring cautiously,
Fire growing bigger,
Dwarfs eyes growing larger,
Fire making spiral patterns,
Trolls spying,
Dying to jump out
to torture the poor dwarfs.

Matthew Selby (10)
Jenner Park Primary School

EARTH

I'm your steps to heaven
No one would live without me
I made water and grass
I'm king of all kingdoms
I'm more exotic than a star
The whistling wind can't blow me
I'm your habitat
I'm your outer skin
All monuments great and small
Are born on me, and die on me
I munch up tiny little seeds
And gobble up graves that are cracked
I breathe your air
The deeper you know me
The more confusing I get.

Scott Jones (11)
Jenner Park Primary School

ALONE

Desolate,
No one to talk to,
No one to be my friend,
The only noise is the constant arguing.
Tears flow down my face
Like a waterfall crashing on the surface.
I can hear my parents hitting the rocks.
Afraid,
Frightened of a divorce.
I'll run away.

Rhian John (11)
Jenner Park Primary School

DEATH

Cold,
Freezing cold,
Body temperature dropping.
Heartbeat slowing down,
59 beats a minute,
58 beats a minute,
Dropping lower and lower.
Pulse faint, slowly getting fainter, fainter,
Symptoms of death.
In the winter I see plants die,
I compare them to myself,
The end is near,
People start to die,
Crops are destroyed,
Land starts to crumble,
Fire eats everything in its path,
Death is upon us.

Logan Saunders (10)
Jenner Park Primary School

THE SEA

Serene
Yet the grave of many
Noisy children play on me
I can be very rough in a storm
I am the centre of the earth
I cloak many things
I'm the habitation of hundreds
I'm the refreshment for umpteen people
I'm the life support system of the planet
I eat the cliffs.

Ellis Mazey
Jenner Park Primary School

NIGHT

Moonlight flooding through the window
I'm staring motionless at the swishing trees
Howling wolves screech and cry
Glittering stars shine over me
Like spirits flowing through my body
I can feel a breeze on my cheek
I'm isolated
The phantom's prisoner
Shadows move around me
Like an Indian tribe
Creepy
Spooky
Soon everything quietens down
It's almost peaceful
All I can hear is owls hooting
I crept towards my cosy bed
I close my tired eyes
Asleep at last.

Holly Miller (11)
Jenner Park Primary School

BEACH

I'm desolate, isolated
I'm marooned on a desert island
My chance of escape was buried deep down under the ocean floor
I thought I would never see civilisation again!
I continued to search for a sign of life
If I don't shout for help now I would be stuck here forever
I smell food from all directions
I feel like an egg in a frying pan.

Louis John Ayres
Jenner Park Primary School

WAVES UPON THE SHORE

Waves splatter their cold spray
against the hot sand,
Gusty wind rushes past like a racing car
completing lap after lap,
Clouds form pictures as they dart
across the breezy sky,
The cold sea ripples and sways like
a pendulum of a grandfather clock,
Waves bubble as they lap against the shore,
The sky changes colour like a chameleon
blending into his surroundings,
A blast of wind blows the sand across
the beach like a whale squirting out air.

Michelle Green (11)
Jenner Park Primary School

SMILE

I cost nothing,
I appear when people are happy
like a spirit rising from the dead.
When you are sad I disappear.
You were born with me.
One sign of fear and I'll disappear
like a happy noise fading away.
I am always there just hiding away
like an animal not wanting to be seen.
One sign of cheer I'll be there
a Jack-in-the-box leaping into the air.
You might be wearing one.
I am the finishing touch of appearance.

Sian Jones (11)
Jenner Park Primary School

BANDIT OF THE NIGHT

Calm
Motionless
Walking through the gloomy woods
I saw a weird figure
Moving through the trees
Glancing at me
With piercing eyes
Looking annoyed
Blood thirsty
Pointing his twig-like fingers
His spiky nose
Making him look deadly
Vicious
The bandit of the night
Reaching for me with his mossy arms
I feel petrified
Scared
Wondering, is it going to catch me.

Michael Cundliffe (10)
Jenner Park Primary School

DARKNESS

I choke the earth like a python killing its prey
I am your worst enemy
I appear where there is no light
I make you nervous
I make you frightened
I come all the time
You can't escape from me
You'll see me every night
You can extinguish me by turning on a light.

Shaun Newman (10)
Jenner Park Primary School

BANDIT OF THE NIGHT

Calm.
Motionless.
The bandit of the night
approaches the wild woods.
His big piercing eyes staring at me
like headlights blinding a petrified rabbit.

His hand reaching towards me
like a prehistoric spider
maniac.

Insane,
mossy skin,
the gloomy woods calm . . .

Kyle Haggarty (11)
Jenner Park Primary School

THE FOREST

Moonlights shadow floating across,
misty clouds,
towering trees with jagged thorns,
inky blackness all around me,
an eerie sound,
the wind like icy fingertips,
brushing across my face,
full moon so bright,
motionless I drift away,
so silent,
an owl hoots shattering the silence.

Stacey Pope (10)
Jenner Park Primary School

STORMY NIGHT

Boom!
Waves crashing against rocks
terrified sailors
flooding streets
people trapped in houses
like insects trapped in webs
trees snapped in half
like old brittle bones
owls hidden in lonely ruins
trying to hide from the storm
Flash!
Lightning terrorising boats
piercing the darkness
lighting up the streets
for a moment
it darts out in all directions
like a firework exploding
in the dark sky.

Michael Osborne (11)
Jenner Park Primary School

THE TOWERS

The white towers
As tall as mountains
Join together with the bright blue sky
Clouds float like gliding birds
The rock twists around like an everlasting spiral
Evening mist creeping up like an army of ghosts.

Christopher Burston (10)
Jenner Park Primary School

WHALES

The lonely little girl sits there
waiting for something to happen.
The black and white whales
surge through the air like the sly
eagle charging at its prey.
The icy waves crash against the
side of the tall, grey cliff.
The mist, dark and menacing
all is so quiet and peaceful
calm but relaxing.
The girl feels settled, confident
she feels she can never leave.
The moonlight set upon her pale
dull face
        setting the scene.

Nicole Kear (11)
Jenner Park Primary School

THE TROLLS

In a dark grey cave
With sunlight peeping in
The hideous monsters hold the poor scared hobbit
By his little, hairy feet,
Over a hot cooking pan.
The trolls have goofy teeth and long fat fingers,
Eyes like bouncy balls,
Huge thin noses.
Their skin is like mashed up cooking foil,
Crinkly and crunchy.
They feel excited,
Ready to eat cooked hobbit flesh.

Abbey Rowlands (10)
Jenner Park Primary School

THE GHOULS' GATHERING

In the dead of night
the witches,
the skeletons,
the ghosts and ghouls
gather together
for their last night of freedom.
They start in the graveyard,
on into the town,
into the city
where the fun begins.
In the city
they scare anyone
who dares to come out
of their houses.
They return to the graveyard,
they rest in their graves
until they are free to go
next All Hallows Eve.

Mary Doyle (10)
Jenner Park Primary School

FANGORN FOREST

The ancient trees stand on the bank of
the fast flowing river
Branches are tangled and twisted like
hair in the morning
Roots grab the ground like claws
Two weary hobbits try to escape from
hundreds of men on horseback
Dashing across fields and into the
forest.

Sylvia Doyle (10)
Jenner Park Primary School

NIENNOR MEETS GLAURUNG THE DRAGON

The sky is clear blue,
The sun is shining,
But young Niennor is as pale as death.
She stands quietly on the high broken cliff.
She gazes into the dragon's eyes.
His teeth are like a row of bread knives,
But young Niennor stays still.
His massive, ugly body curves over the thick, brown grass.
His mouth waters,
But Niennor stays still
Except for her long red hair blowing in the wind.

Samantha Germon & Tabitha Brown (11)
Jenner Park Primary School

MELKOR AND UNGOLIANT

A hidden place in jagged mountains
Melkor and Ungoliant
Making a deal to destroy the world
Melkor, vicious like a starving wolf
Cunning like a fox
Darker than evil.
Ungoliant the gigantic spider,
Taller than a castle
Fiendish,
Sinister.
An opaque mist swirls below
A blood red sky above
Huge shadows perform a diabolical dance
On the mountains
What will happen to the world?

Peter Pearce (10)
Jenner Park Primary School

DRAGON

The evil dragon swiftly swoops down
From the tall jagged cliff
Perches itself steadily
High above the earth
On a rocky mountain peak
It slyly watches it unsuspecting victim
As it walks into its territory.

Then the dragon speeds down
Faster than an arrow
Blocks the terrified victim's path
With a wall of fire.

Still in flight
The dragon stretches its long flexible neck
And with a quick snap of its enormous jaws
The dragon has caught its prey.

Mark Michael Gronow (10)
Jenner Park Primary School

INK PEN

I bleed like deadly poison.
Sometimes I'm the voice of anger.
But other times I express eternal love.
Over the years my appearance has changed.
Sometimes I need a transplant.
It can be one of many colours.
I drift across surfaces like a swan gliding over
a smooth calm lake.
I plan the future and I record the past.

Laura J Hawkins (11)
Jenner Park Primary School

HE NEVER GOES AWAY

A big pair of blood-red eyes
Peering through my bedroom window
Coming closer every time I move
Blinking on and off like two red lightbulbs.

They disappear.

I approach the window
Crawling along the floor like a terrified snake.
I look out carefully.
I hope he's gone.

Suddenly he appears like a black bat
out of the night!
His glowing eyes make me dizzy.
I'm feeling sick and faint.
I fall to the floor and scurry under my bed.
Invisible.

He lives in my attic.
I hear him up there.
He never goes away.
He comes to me every night.
He never goes away.
Never goes away.
Never.

Luke Matthews (10)
Jenner Park Primary School

FAREWELL TO LORIEN

The huge swan drifts gracefully
towards a crowd of dwarfs,
They watch with fascination,
The people reach out to stroke the
soft, white feathers as she goes
past,
The golden leaves fall onto the
reflecting river,
The sweet sound of the harp is
drifting through the air.
There is a beautiful scent of wild
flowers,
The lilies drift across the lake
towards a flock of smaller swans,
Ready to take flight
The clouds are gathering in the
clear blue sky.

Michelle Stanton (10)
Jenner Park Primary School

THE SEA

Sometimes I'm dirty
Sometimes I'm clean
I mix sand and rocks together
I can climb cliffs
I am powerful
You can run into me
I can swallow you and eat you
And I can spit you back out.

Dawn Baker (11)
Jenner Park Primary School

RED EYES AT NIGHT

A pair of red eyes
Like two glaring fireballs
Looking through my bedroom window
Stare at me all night
It growls at me to let it in
But I'm shivering underneath my quilt

It closes its eyes
So I think it's not there
I get up and creep slowly towards the window
I can see my breath on the pane
It suddenly flicks its eyes open
I jump back and gasp
I dive into my bed and swoop under the bedclothes

At night
It's always there
Up against my window
In the day
It lurks in the garden shed
Waiting for the dark to come again.

Kyle Wheeler-Adams (10)
Jenner Park Primary School

CELEBRATION 2000

C elebrate that's what we do
E ating drinking like a zoo
L aughing, we're doing it all night long
E ating until all gone
B anging music against the wall
R inging telephones that's all!
A ngry tempered neighbours
T he party will be in full swing
I will give my mum a ring
O n the night it will be fine
N eighbours said this house is mine.

Jamie Elsworth (8)
Mayhill Junior School

CELEBRATION 2000

Celebrating the year 2000,
It will go with a bang,
People will celebrate with parties,
Children will stay up late,
People will be singing,
Champagne will be popping,
People will be merry
Singing on the streets.

Kimberley L Pearce (98)
Mayhill Junior School

A WORLD OF THE FUTURE

Humans turning into animals because of the
blink of an eye
Go to Mars, travel to the moon
Children don't have to clean their rooms
Cos this is a world of the future.

Have wings, fly through the sky
Ever wish you were a fish?
You can be cos this is a world of the future.

Move things with your mind
Be extremely telepathic.
Life's a breeze you'll never graze your knees
Cos this is a world of the future.

Don't pollute the earth.
You won't have to cut down trees,
You'll have your own paper,
You'll have your own chairs.
There'll be cures for every disease,
No one will ever die
Cos this is a world of the future.

Luke Frost (10)
Overmonnow Primary School

BLACKBERRYING

Blackberries in pies,
Blackberries in tarts,
Blackberries in crumbles,
Blackberries in jams and jellies,
All so nice to eat.

People pick them
In late summer.
They come out
On prickly branches
And all over hedges.

Rebecca Jones (10)
Park Terrace Primary School

BLACKBERRYING

I go out blackberrying,
On late summer days,
'Put your old clothes on!'
My mother says.

I go down the field
And into the park,
I pick some but eat some,
Until it gets dark.

I pick all I like,
Then give them to my mam,
She cleans them and boils them,
Into sweet blackberry jam.

A few days later,
I have some on my toast,
Whenever someone tastes the jam,
I always boast,

'I picked those!'

Jade Charles (11)
Park Terrace Primary School

BLACKBERRYING

They squash in your hands
And stain them,
They get all over your clothes,
Grubs and seeds
Sour and sweet
They squash on your shoes
As you tread on them.

They are sour and sweet
And tasty to eat,
Pick them in late summer
And make yourself a treat.
Picking them is fun,
As they ripen in the sun.

Gemma Blake (11)
Park Terrace Primary School

BLACKBERRYING

We wear old clothes,
To go picking,
We use a stick,
To hit them down,
We use a plastic tub,
To carry them.
We even eat some,
When we pick them,
We like to make pies,
Tarts, crumble and jam,
In August and September.

Eleanor Harris (11)
Park Terrace Primary School

BLACKBERRYING

Blackberries here,
Blackberries there,
Blackberries seem to be,
Everywhere.
In the hedge, down the lane,
The thorns hurt, oh what a pain!

Hedges full of juicy fruit,
It's best not to wear a nice suit,
Because they can stain
And that's a pain.
They are ready
Some time in August and September,
So don't forget because
I remember!

Nisha Evans-Derrick (11)
Park Terrace Primary School

THE DRAGON

Deep in the boiling belly of the countryside,
The dragon monster peeps,
Flashes of boiling fire glow through his teeth,
His eyes are like fireballs glistening,
His tail is like a scarlet snake
Teeth as sharp as glass,
Shining crimson red body settles
Shimmering, blunt scales,
His eyes droop
He is asleep.

Jason Rees (11)
Pen-y-Fro Primary School

THE GHOLASH

Down in the murky waters of Wales,
Lies a gholash, a fierce, brutal beast,
Stamping, smashing, crashing, bashing across the valleys,
Mercilessly devouring cattle.

Petrifying poor peasants, while munching mortals,
His beard is thin and mouldy,
A result of eating shivering sheep and cold cows,
In the Welsh farms.

He is the guardian of Wales,
Fighting dragons, monsters and ogres,
Defending the country
And providing safety for the Welsh people.

Felix Morgan (10)
Pen-y-Fro Primary School

THE GIGANTIC GIANT

A gigantic giant grunts grotesquely,
While staggering down the hill.
The bulky mass of the giant,
Creates havoc in the valley below.
The giant continues on going,
With a growl and a snarl.
He petrifies everyone he meets,
He looks like a rock, bumpy and jagged,
A piece of steel is his belt,
Bent by himself you know.

Geraint Davies (11)
Pen-y-Fro Primary School

THE WELSH DRAGON

The dragon lies sleeping,
His body slouched like a small mountain,
He awakes
And slinks up the hillside,
To stand majestically, guarding.

His body is a scarlet steam engine,
Glistening in the sunlight,
His legs are thick tree trunks covered in blood,
His eyes are two sparkling lakes,
Two smouldering volcanoes for nostrils.

Breathing fire as he signals,
As he stands on the border,
As a warning to all enemies,
Guarding and protecting his country.

Abi Carroll (10)
Pen-y-Fro Primary School

THE DRAGON

The dragon shuffles,
The sound of a machine gun following him.
He is so brave, he is Welsh pride.
He's strong like an ox,
His eyes are fierce, guarding Wales.
His head becomes red during a fight,
He scares away the opponent,
His overlapping scales are crimson red.
His nostrils blow, fire scorching red.

Robert Kirkhouse (11)
Pen-y-Fro Primary School

THE WELSH GIANT

He bellows a voice which booms like thunder,
He jumps gigantic steps, while his legs stretch a mile,
As he trudges through the mud and mess,
Next crawling through the windy grass of the countryside.

His feet are enormous like boulders;
Boots are gigantic rocks in the sea,
He wears ragged clothes and a head all green.

Gruesome, scary Welsh giant,
His blood-covered jacket, soaked and red,
A sharp, frightening spear at his side.

Amy Griffiths (10)
Pen-y-Fro Primary School

THE ENORMOUS GIANT

The gigantic, grumpy giant,
Crawls and stumbles around the countryside.

He's plump, warty and hairy,
Just like an ugly witch.

He enjoys killing bats, mice
And especially nosy kids, devouring them like a lion.

He has emerald eyes and an enormous nose,
His face is as smooth as a piece of paper.

His hair is as soft and shiny
As a dog's coat.

Charlotte Jones (11)
Pen-y-Fro Primary School

THE BFG

Moves like a bear, gracefully he strides,
As huge as a great blue whale,
Friendly as a loving cat.
His football shaped biceps bulge.

Slumbering peacefully as a newborn baby
After the nap, he stumbles out to find a feast
Sheep and cows become his next meal.

As handsome as sleeping beauty's prince,
Ears are those of a little bird,
Eyes gleaming brilliant sapphire blue,
Brilliant blonde hair shines in the sun.

As he steps out of his cave he surveys the mountain
He sees the river trickling down the valley
The view reminds him of why he is the giant of Wales.

Charlie Foulkes (10)
Pen-y-Fro Primary School

THE DRAGON OF WALES

The dragon from Wales breathes fire through his nose,
The dragon has claws as sharp as a dog's teeth,
His teeth are as sharp as a razor's
And dripping with blood.
He is the dragon from Wales
Kind and thoughtful just like us,
The Welsh people.

Rhys Smith (11)
Pen-y-Fro Primary School

RED DRAGON VS WHITE DRAGON

As the dragon walks around the corner,
I notice smoke from his nostrils,
He is enormous and grotesque,
He scares newcomers away,
He crouches at the guard point
And scans the countryside for enemies.
Another dragon approaches the land,
It's the dragon from England.
The Welsh dragon breathes fire like a volcano
Luckily he misses,
The Welsh dragon swoops his tail,
He crops him and rolls down the mountain
Like a large boulder into the swamp,
Super red dragon saves Wales,
The Welsh dragon resumes his place on the mountain
And guards his beloved Wales.

Oliver Corbisiero (11)
Pen-y-Fro Primary School

PIMPO

He sleeps but one day every year,
In his stony, rocky lair,
His pimply head, with lumps and spots,
Rises from his enormous cot.

His broad shoulders rise and fall
His appearance, very tall
A giant belt for a giant belly
He'd sooner sleep than watch the telly.

His muscly legs crash on the ground
And frighten everyone around
With gigantic bats and smelly feet
He knocks out the people he'd like to meet.

Heather Mills (10)
Pen-y-Fro Primary School

THE WELSH DRAGON

You will only see him once a year,
Slithering over the mountains like a snake,
His ears are pointed arrow heads
And his eyes are glistening lakes.

He moves slowly, purposefully, threateningly
Across the gigantic hill.
He opens his mouth to reveal his huge teeth
Ready for his next kill.

His skin looks wet and slimy,
With his large scarlet scales,
His back is curved like a colourful rainbow,
Which soon becomes his tail.

He only stirs on the first of March,
To commemorate St David's Day.
As soon as that day has nearly passed,
He trudges home, and once again, he lays.

Lara Amber Roberts (11)
Pen-y-Fro Primary School

THE DRAGON

I climbed upon the hill
And crept beside the cave.
I saw it snoring silently,
Slouching upon the stones.

With eyelids covering fireballs,
His scaly skin scratches
And he grinds his fierce teeth.

His boiling body bulges slowly,
His trudging tail follows on behind,
His snaky skin continues his scaly skin.

He trudges towards the valleys,
Causing chaos as he walks,
Off to guard his country,
While people go freakily home.

He returns to his lair,
Settles his humungous body
and falls asleep again
I creep inside to make his acquaintance
And close my eyes.

Ria Davies (10)
Pen-y-Fro Primary School

A BLANKET OF ICE

It is icy outside,
Children skidding and sliding.
It is as white as a pillow,
As cold as an ice-cream.
It is really good fun to play on the ice,
It is crystal clear.

Leaves and grass are solid,
Frost on houses and sheds.
The sun is cold
People wrapping up warm to play
The frost is as light as a feather
And the ice is as white as can be.

Kristy Jones (10)
St Alban's RC Primary School, Pontypool

WAR

I can't imagine
I try
Black clothes
Blood
People die.

I try
Hideous
Dangerous and hell
Bombs exploding
Grown men crying
Heartbreaking.

War is hopeless
Pointless
Why?
People so frightened
Lives so shattered
Dreams in pieces
I can't imagine.

Laura Bisset (11)
St Alban's RC Primary School, Pontypool

MY HOUSE

Out in the breeze on a summer's day
A smell of sweet smelling hay,
Hung in the air,
Hovering in fields where it lay.

The stream trickles down the hill
Down to the water wheel by the mill.
The cats are catching mice
And lining them up on the windowsill.

The horses are being led,
The pigs are in the shed.
The cows are being milked,
And the lambs are being fed!

Lisa Bisset (11)
St Alban's RC Primary School, Pontypool

I AM

I am thwacking my tail in the sunset ocean
Whirling, twirling and plunging.
I plunge in the deep seas
I twirl like a ballet dancer.
I whirl around as happy as a nightingale
Gliding like an ice-skater.
I see my family as I head towards the Photic Zone
I see microscopic fish as if they were visible
My brothers and sisters go away
As I turn to my pod.

Kerry-Ann Jenkins (11)
St Alban's RC Primary School, Pontypool

FROST ON THE YARD

As I wake in the morning frost
I look at it
It twinkles at me and glitters
Sliding and slipping
Clear blue skies
As I walk into school
I see all children
I hate the snow I think I will slip
Especially if my laces are undone
I think I will trip
Solid leaves, frozen twigs
Cold as ice-cream
Shiver and chilled
I look to the floor white as a pillow
The frost is shining
My shadow is long
I wonder if I will slip if I walk along.

Laura-Kate Reed (9)
St Alban's RC Primary School, Pontypool

NIGHT

The night is dark and cold like a cave deep underground,
The stars twinkle and glitter as bright as diamonds,
The moon is big and shiny like a giant snowball,
The wind rustles and howls like a wolf,
Some animals go to sleep,
The petals on the flowers close up like a wound healing,
Owls come out hooting while everyone else is asleep.

Joseph Bold (10)
St Alban's RC Primary School, Pontypool

THE OCEAN

The ocean is wild,
It's faster than the wind.
Its waves are as big as mountains
And it's stronger than a beast.
It explores the world
And its waves crash against the rocks.

Sometimes the waves are so strong,
They crash down on the rocks,
Especially when a storm comes,
The ocean roars like mad,
It is madder than all the prides
Put together.

It roars so loud that houses crash down,
The waves cover the land,
Then sun is rising and the ocean is calm,
Nearly everything is destroyed.

Emily Price (9)
St Alban's RC Primary School, Pontypool

MISS AND ME

It's the beginning of the week
And I'm raring to go
I'm full of enthusiasm
And Miss shouts 'Oh no!'

I'm terribly clumsy
Over all things I fall
I'm like Bambi on ice
So flighty and tall.

It's the end of the day
Miss lets out a sigh
The class is all empty
We've said our goodbyes.

The week is over
I've done my best
But my teacher - her patience
I've put to the test.

Madilyn Smith (11)
St Alban's RC Primary School, Pontypool

UNDER THE SEA

I am the one who lives under the sea
I swim over the Photic Zone,
The plants tickling my tummy
With Mum and Dad,
I am only a pup.

I swim with Mum and we thwack our tails
I sometimes swim with the dolphins
We sing our favourite songs to each other.

I like to swim towards the sunset
I like doing flips
My favourite food is plankton
I like cuttlefish too
I swim round with my mouth open
Eating the microscopic fish

I also like to whirl with the dolphins
For they are my only friends.

Sarah Felvus (10)
St Alban's RC Primary School, Pontypool

WAR

People wearing gas masks when the sirens go
Rushing to the shelters the nearest one to you
Food being rationed we can't have as much to eat
Bombs falling, people running to the shelters.

Children being evacuated from London to Wales
They're afraid abut leaving they don't want to go
They wish they could go back home,
Back to London,
Back to Mum,
But they can't go back because of the war
War is sad.

Nicola Day (11)
St Alban's RC Primary School, Pontypool

AS WHITE AS A PILLOW

As white as a pillow
Jack Frost on the grass
When I step on the grass it crunches
Frosted leaves everywhere
Clear blue skies glittering and like crystal
My breath is cold as an iceberg
When I stand I slide and slip
I shiver.

Lindsey Steed (10)
St Alban's RC Primary School, Pontypool

MY FANTASY DREAM

In the land that I would want,
There would be a chocolate font,
In my world of fantasy,
There would be a candy tree.

It's never night it's always day,
So that I can always play,
As I look all around,
There's minty grass on the ground.

In this paradise where I live,
All dogs would talk and cats would fly,
The birds speak as they waddle by.

I climb to the top of the mountain,
Which is made of strawberry icing,
I jump off my wafer diving board,
Into my banana fountain,
As I swim to the banana falls,
I see my chocolate Malteser ball.

Now it's time for me to rest,
In my minty bubblegum nest,
I shut my eyes and go to sleep
Oh what's that I hear, a beep,
It's my alarm it's time to get up,
Now I'm really fed up.

Oh well it was all a dream,
Mum's calling me for breakfast
And I bet it's not ice-cream.

Kirsty Kitchener (10)
St Alban's RC Primary School, Pontypool

CELEBRATION 2000

Bong! The clock strikes twelve,
It is the dawning of the new millennium,
Fireworks, like multicoloured stars explode,
In the pitch black sky.

Everyone is cheering and drinking champagne,
'Happy New Year!' some of them shout,
Little children go to bed, after the long wait
And dream about the next day.

Computers have survived the crash,
They still work when they are switched on,
But will they survive the next time round?
Some wonder.

People all over Britain celebrate in their own style,
They do as they like,
There is no crime on this evening
And no one gets arrested.

But what is happening?
Things aren't like they used to be,
Everyone is living in the Stone Age,
Now modern things are taking over!

People are losing their jobs,
This is a disaster!
New vehicles for different purposes,
What an awful year.

What happened to celebration 2000?

Alex Fisher (10)
St David's CW Primary School, Cowbridge

CELEBRATION 2000!

In the year 2000,
People will start again,
Robots will do all the hard work
And humans will just leave it to them!

The world will take a step in advancement,
Computers will become man's best friend,
They'll invent a cure for cancer
And global warming will come to an end!

People will start to realise,
The state their world is in,
They'll clear up all the rubbish
And put it in a litter bin!

Animals will make an advancement,
Sheep will learn how to swim,
You'll be able to chat with a cow,
And fish won't be so dim!

Robert Anderson (10)
St David's CW Primary School, Cowbridge

CELEBRATION 2000

In a whole year's time,
a new baby will be in its cot.
We will also be in the year two thousand,
whether you like it or not!

In London they're building a Millennium Dome,
it's fit for a king to sit on his throne.
People say it's a big waste of money,
But I think it's all exciting and funny.

On New Year's Eve 1999
most people will be celebrating and drinking wine.
Even though some people will be fast asleep,
the magic of the millennium they will still keep!

Kate Marples (11)
St David's CW Primary School, Cowbridge

THE RED HELL

As red as hot, breathing fire on bonfire night,
As red as streaming thick blood,
As red as ginger hair swiftly moving in the night,
As red as a gleaming ruby on a finger.

As red as anger in someone's heart,
As red as a dragon full of evil,
As red as a ribbon wrapped over a parcel,
As red as the devil in his home.
        The red *hell!*

Kayleigh Owen (9)
St Gwlady's Junior School, Bargoed

ALL AROUND ME

All around me are . . .
Morning sounds
Noisy tele playing
Yawning parents waking
Big bacon sizzling

School sounds
Junior children working
Grey sparrows singing
Small teachers talking.

Night sounds
Brown owls hooting
Black dogs barking
Yellow stars twinkling.

Hannah Banks (8)
St Gwlady's Junior School, Bargoed

SAD I AM

I am a video without any tape,
I am a Tarzan without an ape,
I am a fire without a flame,
I am a boy that gets the blame.
I am a substation without any power
I am an orange and I am sour.
I am a sander without any wood
I am a boy and I'm never good.
My name is Mitchell Lloyd Ryan
I go to Saint Glawdys School, Bargoed.

Mitchell Ryan (11)
St Gwlady's Junior School, Bargoed

ALL AROUND ME

Morning sounds
All around me are . . .

Sleepy children waking,
Sizzling bacon frying
Brown toast heating.

School sounds
All around me are . . .

Screeching pencils writing
Squeaking chairs moving
Scrunched paper in bin.

Home sounds
All around me are . . .

White iron ironing
Brown coffee heating
Cream tea eaten.

Alex Meade (8)
St Gwlady's Junior School, Bargoed

EASTER BONNETS

Easter bonnets, there they are,
Big and small, tiny and tall,
With flowers, bears and chocolate wares,
Magicians' hats that are full of surprises
They make you laugh, they make you stare
They make you glad that Easter's here.

Samantha Williams (10)
St Gwlady's Junior School, Bargoed

SIMILES

As red as an apple
Shiny and juicy
As green as the mountainside grass
Growing in the autumn sun
As blue as the water
That sparkles and glistens
As black as the darkness of night
As black as the soot on my shoe
As loud as the roaring thunder
As loud as a trumpet long and thin
As fast as a car racing a motor bike
As fast as a bird flying in the air
As slow as a worm coming down a hill
As slow as a rising flower growing proudly.

Georgina Jenkins (8)
St Gwlady's Junior School, Bargoed

WHEN I GO TO BED AT NIGHT

When I go to bed at night
It's not just to rest my sleepy head
I read books and write
But when I go to sleep
I dream of magic and fantasies
And lots lots more.
When I go to bed at night
It's not just to rest my sleepy head
I have different kinds of *fun.*

Rhiannon Walters (10)
St Gwlady's Junior School, Bargoed

SIMILES

As blue as the sea
Shining and deep.
As red as an apple
Shiny, red and juicy
As green as the mountain grass.
As black as night
Dark and still.
As white as the Holy Ghost.
As yellow as the bright sun
Shining and hot
As loud as thunder
Banging and shaking
As fast as a motor bike.

Natasha Moore (9)
St Gwlady's Junior School, Bargoed

SIMILES

As old as a steam train, dusty and smelling of smoke.
As red and as sticky as blood.
As black and as messy as coal.
As blue as the sky in daylight.
As s-l-o-w and as green as a turtle.
As fast as a racing car racing in a rally.
As mad as a Tasmanian devil.
As black as a tunnel echoing around.
As fierce and as strong as a boxer.
As orange and as bright as the sun.

Jamie Ford & Lewis Rogers (8)
St Gwlady's Junior School, Bargoed

CRASHING!

Waves crashing on the rocks
Bonfires exploding in the sky
Whirlwinds twisting in the black night
Armies shooting guns up into space
Lightning flashing into the moonlight
Something flies across the moon
A loud howl comes from somewhere
As the sun comes out all of this mystery fades away
       into
          a
             different
                world.

Helen Russell (8)
St Gwlady's Junior School, Bargoed

MINIBEAST

It flutters through the air
like an angel
and stings like
a snake
Black and yellow coat
is danger
It eats honey for
its tummy
when it goes into a flower
Have you guessed yet?
It's a
Bumblebee.

Jonathan Phillips (9)
St Gwlady's Junior School, Bargoed

SOUNDS AROUND US

Car crashing in the street
people talking in the shop
people walking through the town
birds singing in the park.

Leaves swirling on the ground
wind blowing all around
children down by the stream
dragonflies fluttering about.

Cows mooing all day long
grass swaying in the field
bells ringing from the church
bees buzzing everywhere.

Children shouting
trees blowing from side to side
people talking to the
keeper of the shop
then the door slams *shut!*

Emma Pritchard (8)
St Gwlady's Junior School, Bargoed

AS GREEN AS

As green as grass on a spring morning.
As green as stems on a rose.
As green as leaves on a spiky twig.
As green as the cats' eyes glaring up at me.
As green as trees on a cold day.
As green as apples on a golden day.

Jenna Yates (8)
St Gwlady's Junior School, Bargoed

PARTY TIME

It's that time of night
And there's a beautiful sight.
We are hiding in the house that isn't very nice
And we are quiet as little mice.
Then the door opens and we all jump out
And shout . . .
            Surprise
I am not in the mood
To have any food
There are lots of buffoons
And plenty of balloons.
The light went off
And in flew a moth
And we all screamed . . .
            Run

Kirsty McKay (10)
St Gwlady's Junior School, Bargoed

MINIBEAST

A minute leaf floating in the warm sunny air.
Beautiful and colourful.
It is symmetrical.
Lovely wings fluttering.
Two long antennae.
Loves the smell of roses.
It is a minibeast.
It's a beautiful butterfly.

Rachael Roach (9)
St Gwlady's Junior School, Bargoed

SIMILES

As red as an apple, shiny and juicy.
As green as paint, wet and sticky.
As blue as the sea, shining in the sun.
As black as night, dark and spooky.
As *loud* as drums and disco music.
As fast as the howling, powerful,
Thunderous wind.
As s-l-o-w as the lazily smooth clouds.
As cold as the frosty snowflakes falling
From the sky.
As old as the sun living before time.
As small as a tiny little minibeast.

Andrew Ashcroft (8)
St Gwlady's Junior School, Bargoed

MINIBEASTS

It is an angel
flying through the sky.
It has symmetrical wings
floating like a leaf
down down it goes onto a
flower.
Have you guessed?
     It
          is
               a
                    butterfly.

Brett Jones (8)
St Gwlady's Junior School, Bargoed

MINIBEASTS

It is like a mini monster
crawling across the floor.
It is really hairy and
it's really small.
It has two fangs to
bite with.
It moves around like
a baby.
And it moves
very fast.
it is like a mini monster
I think it's a spider.

Andrew Ashcroft (8)
St Gwlady's Junior School, Bargoed

MINIBEASTS

They look like a
Tiger
they sound like a
Helicopter buzzing
they have two pairs
of wings
it likes to make
Honey
it only stings
when somebody
disturbs it.
What is it?
A bumblebee.

Jamie Ford (9)
St Gwlady's Junior School, Bargoed

MINIBEAST

It flies in the
Beautiful air.
It has beautiful
wings with
lovely patterns
like a pretty
leaf floating
in the clean
air it is a
beautiful
butterfly
flying
in the
air.

Laura Carter (9)
St Gwlady's Junior School, Bargoed

MARS

I am Mars, the god of war.
I dress in a red cloak.
On my head is a heavy golden helmet.
My eyes are like red hot volcanoes.
My voice is like booming thunder.
My breath is like strong garlic.
I like to hear the clanging of swords.
I love to see people dying in pain.
My friends are Jupiter, Pluto and
The roaring volcanoes.

Hywel Matthews (9)
St Gwlady's Junior School, Bargoed

WHAT'S THAT CLOUD

Clouds white, puffy, clear
Clouds here, there, everywhere!
Clouds shaped like the sea
So you and me can play clouds

Cumulus puffy around the top
Cumulonimbus a big giant
Rolling a dark rock.

Altocumulus a middle cloud that
Is thinner, patchy and rippled.
Nimbostratus a dark raining cloud
That brings rain.

Then into the night time
The clouds are gone
but tomorrow they come again
So we can do it once again.

Natalie Bressington (10)
St Gwlady's Junior School, Bargoed

MINIBEAST

Floating in the air
Like an autumn leaf
It has beautiful
wings and it has
patterns on it.
It is a
gliding, gliding
                    butterfly
          Gentle and calm.

Natasha Marie Moore (9)
St Gwlady's Junior School, Bargoed

SOUNDS AROUND ME

Thunder booming
Rain splashing
In the sky
Bang!

Car booming
Children banging
In the street
Crash!

Ants scurrying
Birds tweeting
In the forest
Splash!

TV blaring
Stereo humming
In the house
Stop!

Sarah Cullum (8)
St Gwlady's Junior School, Bargoed

FLUTTER BY BUTTERFLY

Beautiful butterfly
Under the flowers
They go in trees
They flutter their wings to fly
Everywhere they fly
Round the trees
Flying butterfly
Leaps up into the sky
Yellow butterfly.

Stephanie Griffiths (8) & Christie Evans
St Gwlady's Junior School, Bargoed

THE CLIMBING BOY

Some of them get stuck between the bricks
Some dead, some alive.
Every day a danger,
No rights for these young lads.
Some hide in the trees and weep.
Dirty, cold, hungry and beaten,
Fighting for life.
Every day, every night,
Climbing.
Knees and elbows all at work.
Used to the blood,
Used to the master's call,
Voice inside him telling him to carry on.

Emily Hankins (10)
St Gwlady's Junior School, Bargoed

FLUTTER BY BUTTERFLY

Beautiful butterfly
Under leaves,
Taste
Tasting
Low round
Fluttering
Lands,
You like
Butterflies . . . yes.

Ricky Winston (8) & Ricky Robinson
St Gwlady's Junior School, Bargoed

SOUNDS AROUND US

Car zooming
Door slams shut
Boy shouting in the yard
Boosh!

TV blaring
Stereo blasting
Kettle hooting
Stop!

Chalk squealing
Teacher shouting
In the classroom
Scream!

Ants scuttling
Birds twittering
In the woods
Clam!

Christopher Wynn (8)
St Gwlady's Junior School, Bargoed

AS RED AS . . .

As red as a leaf in the winter.
As red as a berry on a berry bush.
As red as a ladybird in flight.
As red as tomato ketchup all over chips.
As red as an angry dragon.
As red as a lovely rose in the sun.
As red as strawberry jam all over sandwich.
As red as blood on your angry face.
As red as a tomato all sliced up.

Stuart E Jones (9)
St Gwlady's Junior School, Bargoed

Sounds Around Me

Door slams shut!
Watch tick-tock
In my house
In school.

Horse clippedy clops
Book slams shut
Outside
Inside.

Rain splashing
Wind blows
Inside
Outside.

Tiger roars
Crocodile snaps
In the wild
In the zoo.

Christie Evans (8)
St Gwlady's Junior School, Bargoed

As Green As

As green as a bushy tree
As green as a leaping frog
As green as a small leaf
As green as a slippery lizard
As green as a sweet apple
As green as the short cut grass
As green as a felt-tip pen
As green as a bushy cabbage.

Luke Bye (8)
St Gwlady's Junior School, Bargoed

A FROSTY MORNING

I look through my window
cold and bleak
Jack Frost has been
three times this week

The twinkling sun
might make my day
trying to melt
the ice away

A tree is so bare
stretches its wings to the sky
crystal glass icicles
hang twinkling so high

Spider webs sparkle
like tinsel to me
a frosty morning
wonderful to see.

Ryan Woods (10)
St Gwlady's Junior School, Bargoed

AS YELLOW AS . . .

As yellow as the sun gazing down on the earth.
As yellow as wet paint on the wall.
As yellow as a bee in the air.
As yellow as a daffodil in the sunshine.
As yellow as the stars in the sky.
As yellow as the lava coming from a volcano.

Lara Williams (8)
St Gwlady's Junior School, Bargoed

A FROSTY MORNING

On a frosty morning
Ice patterns on my window pane
Outside it was freezing
It felt like a cane
The trees were so bare
With fingers stretching out
No leaves were on there
Winter's here no doubt.

Icicles hang so pretty to see
Cobwebs are like lace.
Fragile and delicate it seemed to me
It's a wonderful place to be.

Bethan Francis (10)
St Gwlady's Junior School, Bargoed

A FROSTY MORNING

The morning is a crystallised sight,
There are icicles hanging from our porch,
Like teeth inside an open mouth,
As the sun is rising, the silhouette
Of the trees are like twisted bodies
The cobwebs are like diamond encrusted tiaras,
When I look at the grass it looks like winter scattered crystals over it
The sun is coming up,
The sky turns pink,
It is time for winter to return to its ice castle
And then winter waits,
He waits for another morning to freeze.

Michael Hollifield (10)
St Gwlady's Junior School, Bargoed

As Red As . . .

As red as a crab on a hot sunny day.
As red as a hot fire blazing on a tree.
As red as an apple shiny and ripe.
As red as roses standing in a vase.
As red as lava running down a mountain.

Alysha Davies (9)
St Gwlady's Junior School, Bargoed

The Attic

In a dark and dusty attic,
Creepy and cold
I look up in the darkness and
I see a spider spinning a crystal web.
It was swaying in the breeze
Scuttling like a snowflake in the sky,
Falling like the soft rain.

Melanie Cook (10)
St Gwlady's Junior School, Bargoed

The Attic

A creepy, murky, old room,
Full of spiders scurrying along
Silently spinning webs.
Battered old suitcases
Crammed with childhood memories.
In the darkness of the room,
Mice are chewing old soft toys.

Anthony Pitt (10)
St Gwlady's Junior School, Bargoed

The Climbing Boy

The climbing boy looked up
At the sooty gloom of the winding chimney
Rats and mice lurking
His knees and elbows grazed and bleeding
Not able to wash.
His thin arms and shaky legs
Working their way up and up
His master waiting
Ready to beat his raw hands.
Starving and cold.
What a horrible, wretched life.

Bethan Stone (10)
St Gwlady's Junior School, Bargoed

Bonfire Night

In the midnight air I see,
A banger, a rocket and a wheel,
The Catherine wheel flicks sparks from it
And all the pretty colours are revealed.

The rocket shoots up and burst right out,
When I look its way
I see every colour that bursts out
You can't really see in the day.

Carys Vaughan (9)
St Helen's RC Junior School, Barry

BONFIRE NIGHT

Bang, boom, burst and pop go the fireworks at night.
The rockets screech and burst.
Bright gleamy and mixed colours come out of it.
Showers of sparks come down and spread
all over the land.
Sparklers are like magic wands
with fireballs on.
They all have rainbow colours and explosions.
I like it a lot, I like it a lot and
I wish it was every day.

Christopher Morgan (9)
St Helen's RC Junior School, Barry

COLOUR PATTERN

Red is the devil,
waiting in hell,
fire is often used, people tell.
Red is a sign of anger
that burns inside.
Red is an apple,
a holly berry too,
but also part of a rainbow
looking down on you.

Michael Berndt (9)
St Helen's RC Junior School, Barry

THE MULTICOLOURED HOOP

The rainbow
is a lovely, circular
multicoloured   hoop
Red is the colour of dark tomato soup
Orange is the colour of the setting sun
Yellow is the sun when the day's begun
Blue is the high summer sky,
Indigo, a lovely show,
Violet, beautiful.

The rainbow!

Rhys Dumbleton (10)
St Helen's RC Junior School, Barry

THE SHINIEST APPLE

In
the
brown big bowl
lies the shiniest apple.
It gleams like a clear crystal.
The apple is as green and shiny
as an emerald. The apple looks like it's
been polished about six times a day.
All the time when I look
in the bowl it shines.

Lauren Furnish (10)
St Helen's RC Junior School, Barry

WHAT IS WHITE?

White is snow on house tops at night,
White is the colour you go when you see a scary sight.
White is the colour when ice covers the ground,
White is the colour of the ghost that haunts our town.
White's the colour that turns black to grey,
White's the colour of the notes that we play.
White's not in the rainbow but is if colours get mixed,
White is the pumps when they get fixed.

Sophie Campbell (9)
St Helen's RC Junior School, Barry

MILLENNIUM

The millennium is approaching
Get ready!

The Millennium Dome is opening
Get ready!

The bells are ringing
Get ready!

The Millennium Bug is approaching
Get ready!

The fireworks are coming
Get ready!

Have fun, get ready for the parties of 2000.

Kelly Ann Williams (11)
St Joseph's RC Primary School, Clydach

DOGS

My dog's names are Lucy and Spot
The one called Spot barks a lot.
Lucy is calm and always quiet
Until Spot fights and starts a riot
When they are fighting they don't stop
Until my father comes out and shouts 'Stop!'

Victoria Williams (11)
St Joseph's RC Primary School, Clydach

MILLENNIUM

People singing and dancing in the night,
All the foxes and badgers are out of sight.
Fireworks are going
And the weather is snowing.
When the night is over,
I drive off in my Rover
Back home
To the Millennium Dome.

Gabrielle Barrett (11)
St Joseph's RC Primary School, Clydach

MILLENNIUM

Millennium is the time for food and wine.
You like it so do I.
Fire is burning really bright,
Just like the millennium light.
Millennium is all about laughter and joy,
Fun for girls and fun for boys.

Marie O'Malley (10)
St Joseph's RC Primary School, Clydach

MILLENNIUM DOME

Millennium Dome, Millennium Dome,
Parties, celebrations and lots of fun.
Millennium Dome, Millennium Dome,
With the shining sun.

Millennium Dome, Millennium Dome,
Still in the stages of building, or was.
Millennium Dome, Millennium Dome,
Champagne, food, are all mine and yours.

Millennium Dome, Millennium Dome,
Opening in the year 2000
Millennium Dome, Millennium Dome,
Opens with thousands and thousands of people.

Louise Wiltshire (10)
St Joseph's RC Primary School, Clydach

MILLENNIUM

Beer, port and some old wine,
Waiting for the millennium to go by

A bottle of wine
A pint of beer
A shandy lager
A Bacardi Breezer

Dazzling, gleaming
Glowing bright
Glittering sparkling
Millennium night.

Victoria Jones (11)
St Joseph's RC Primary School, Clydach

APRIL

April's my horse, I love her a lot,
First we start walking, then into a trot.
I give her some bread and a piece of bun
Then we go off and have some fun.
Galloping away as fast as we can,
I can safely say I'm April's biggest fan.
Jumping over the fence and walls
She's such a good horse, she never falls.
I'd love to keep her for ever and ever,
And if someone asked to buy her I'd say
                                    'No, never!'
She is the colour of the golden sand
And she's worth all the money in the land.
She is better than all the rest
She is better and the *b e s t!*

Hayley Louise Codd (11)
St Joseph's RC Primary School, Clydach

MILLENNIUM

M assive parties will be happening.
I   can't wait for it to happen.
L ots of people and
L ots of wine.
E ntering the Millennium Dome
N oises from the fireworks
N o sleping tonight
I   nside my bedroom.
U ntil my mum comes up and tells
        me to join in with the
M illennium.

Josie Davies (11)
St Joseph's RC Primary School, Clydach

THE BEST MUM AND DAD

I have the best mum and dad,
They are hardly really ever sad.
My dad is always up for pool,
My mum always thinks she's cool.
Not one of them is at all fat,
But once they bought me a big fat cat!
But the thing I like about them most,
Is that they make the finest toast.

Rhodri Clancy (9)
St Joseph's RC Primary School, Clydach

FOOD

F is for food we love to eat
O is for orange I don't like
O is for oysters I still don't like
D is for duck that is meat.

Gareth Harris (10)
St Joseph's RC Primary School, Clydach

TELEPHONES

Telephones come in all different sizes
                    and colours too.
You can carry some telephones around,
And it might only cost you a pound.
So don't delay, just buy one today
And it will make you happy and gay.

Emma Charles (11)
St Joseph's RC Primary School, Clydach

THE MILLENNIUM

There was once a Millennium Bug,
Who lived in the Millennium Dome,
She liked to sing,
She liked to play,
She liked to make a mess,
She liked to crawl sometimes,
She even liked to dance,
She liked to stay up late
              especially on a Saturday,
She would go out every weekday
              especially on a Monday.

Victoria Martin (10)
St Joseph's RC Primary School, Clydach

CHOCOLATE

Crunching, munching away
at my chocolate bar,
gulping it down,
as fast as a Formula 1 car.
Chewing into it,
yum, yum!
Tasting it bit by bit
until it's finally finished.
I crush it up,
throw it up,
and volley it into the bin.

Joseph Williams (10)
St Joseph's RC Primary School, Clydach

BONNIE

My auntie had a dog called Bonnie,
She was cute and very small
She loved playing with her ball,
When I was little, she used to bite me
I was very scared.
When I used to go up her house
I used to run around crying.

One day my auntie said she was moving
I was so sad but then I found out
That she was moving near me
Which wasn't so bad.

I used to take her out for walks
We became very close.
It was one of the happiest times of my life
One day she went missing for hours and hours
But to me it seemed like days and days.
We found her dead.
'At least she's safe' I said.

Claire Brunton (9)
St Joseph's RC Primary School, Clydach

WHALE

W is for *w*hales that are big and blue
H is for *h*umpback I saw in the zoo.
A is for *a*board the ships they are hauled
L is for *l*ovely by some people they are called.
E is for *e*xist which they do and will forever.

Gina Earland (10)
St Joseph's RC Primary School, Clydach

THE PURPLE ALIEN

I have a purple alien
he is short and slimy
with scaly skin.

The purple alien has
three eyes so he
can see triple of me.

When it gets dark and
I am cosy in my
warm, warm bed

I can feel skin
along the floor and
his bones clicking on the door.

Click! Click! Click!

He tries as hard as he can
to scare me off

And he thinks the house
is all his

And when he tries to get
out he scratched his claws
on the glass and on the wall

As hard as possible but no
matter what he does,
he can't get out.

Christina Edwards (9)
St Joseph's RC Primary School, Clydach

MY GOLDFISH

My goldfish is so very small,
And his bowl, well it's so very tall.
He swims all day and sleeps all night,
He really is my true delight.

I named my goldfish Coco,
After a clown I saw in a photo.
I always feed him twice a day,
And with him I really like to play.

Jennifer Lloyd (10)
St Joseph's RC Primary School, Clydach

GHOSTS

Do you believe in ghosts?
They twirl around posts.
Do you believe in ghosts?
That send you little notes.
Do you believe in ghosts?
They sometimes take your coats.
Do you believe in ghosts?
They really do try their most.
Do you believe in ghosts?
They try to make toast.

Laura Jones (10)
St Joseph's RC Primary School, Clydach

PEPSI

Pepsi was my pet
Lop-Eared rabbit he was
He was kind, loving and friendly
Then one day he was gone
The first day that I saw him
I was not aware
That one day it would be so unfair.
We tried to make him better.
Then the night came that my dad and brother
Were going to treat him
Like having lots of fun.
It was too late for that
He had already gone
But I'm glad to know
He had lived quite long.

Katia Philip (9)
St Joseph's RC Primary School, Clydach

SUNFLOWERS

Sunflowers, sunflowers,
how lovely they grow,
With glowing honeysuckle petals
and long green stalks.
Sunflowers, sunflowers,
in the midday sun
Gazing into space at the world to come.

Bridget Thomas (10)
St Joseph's RC Primary School, Clydach

THE WOLF

I try to walk a footstep further
But the wolf lurks in the shadows
Waiting to pounce
He grows with the shadows as night comes on
And I stand there my blood growing colder and colder
The wolf gets bigger as my fears increase
I want to run, but cannot
The glint in his greedy eyes rooting me to the spot
And my courage slithers away silently.
The wolf crawls stealthily towards me
I twitch
Fighting the impulse to run
Just when I begin to control myself
I run over the bumps, running and running
The wolf of my fears runs on two legs
An unearthly being from another world.
I reach the door handle
The wolf leaps!
I rush inside
He scratches and whines at the door
And the glint in his eyes and the wicked grin on his face
Tells me that he'll get me the next time.

Jenny Rickson (10)
St Joseph's RC Primary School, Clydach

MILLENNIUM

Some days,
When I go to school,
The teacher always says,
Millennium Dome is really cool.

Miss talks about Olympics,
Miss talks about education,
Miss talks about the eclipse,
And, the celebration.

Emma Louise Brown (10)
Sudbrook Primary School

MILLENNIUM DOME OPEN

M illennium Bug affects
I deas for the year 2000.
L ife in the future will be good.
L iving in the new year.
E clipse in August.
N ew year finally comes.
N ew days might start.
I mportant messages on the news.
U K currency changes.
M illennium celebrates the day.

D ifferent houses start to change,
O nce the century comes as well.
M illions of people will celebrate.
E ducation will start again.

O lympics start again in summer,
P utting hard work into winning.
E lectric lets the lights come on.
N ever let the good things change

Hannah Wooton (11)
Sudbrook Primary School

MILLENNIUM

M illennium is coming,
I am happy.
L ittle lights flickering
L ittle brothers screaming.
E at the food
N an's kissing everybody.
N ine dads dancing
I' m getting ready to party.
U ncles are going nuts,
M um is cooking a meal.

D ad is drunk.
O ne minute to millennium,
M odel of a human,
E ngineers working.

Scott David Ball (10)
Sudbrook Primary School

MILLENNIUM

M illennium Dome,
I s great and really fun.
L oads of activities to do,
L earn about the year 2000,
E xciting times,
N ew year has come.
N ew start to life.
I deas are coming to the world,
U nderstanding the new future,
M illennium is here!

Matthew Shaun Counsell (10)
Sudbrook Primary School

MILLENNIUM

The millennium is coming;
It is time to celebrate.
Just think it's just a year away,
But I can hardly wait.

Party poppers popping,
It's time to celebrate.
Just think, having a Millennium Dome
And the Olympics in Sydney.

What about ten days in a week,
When we are in school instead of,
Having two days off, five days off school.
Hurrah for the future.

Claire Janine Bishop (9)
Sudbrook Primary School

MILLENNIUM

C ome and look at the new year.
E njoy it a lot, it is great.
L ook around, people celebrating.
E arth is new and better.
B ritain is brighter and new,
R ebuilding the Earth year 2000.
A ctivity in the new UK.
T he companies shutting down,
I nside pubs are the people.
O h now, the night is over.
N ew year is here!

Oliver Hoppis (9)
Sudbrook Primary School

MILLENNIUM

M illennium 2000 coming near,
I deas are building up.
L ike the Dome or not,
L ots and lots of rooms.
E clipse came in August.
N ew Millennium Dome in year 2000.
N ew games, houses and lots more.
I t will be a fabulous place,
U se many lights, nice colourful pictures.
M ight get lost.

D ome is big and huge,
O pen to all visitors.
M illennium Bug *beware!*
E njoy the millennium.

Samantha Norton (9)
Sudbrook Primary School

MILLENNIUM

M aking a Dome,
I nteresting things happening.
L isten to the music,
L ook at the dancing,
E vening celebration,
N ight-time dancing,
N ew shops and towns,
I n the morning.
U K is celebrating,
M illennium is here.

Katie Louise Williams (9)
Sudbrook Primary School

MILLENNIUM

M oving on to the millennium
I n the year 2000.
L ots of laughter,
L ots of singing,
E venings to enjoy
N ights to have fun.
N ew year is coming
I nteresting to see
U nited States is celebrating
M illennium Dome 2000!

Lauren Williams (10)
Sudbrook Primary School

MILLENNIUM

M y first celebration,
I' m looking forward to seeing it.
L ights are shining,
L ives are so happy.
E vening darkness,
N ight is coming.
N aughty people drink too much,
I' ve always seen people happy.
U nlock the doors to see the lights,
M um and Dad go for a drink.

Aimee Jones (9)
Sudbrook Primary School

MILLENNIUM

M any things to see,
I nside and out.
L ots of celebration,
L ots of funny things,
E ducation for all,
N ot to be missed.
N ever to be forgotten,
I n this great Dome,
U nless you're like
M e, I'd rather stay at home.

Catherine Morris (9)
Sudbrook Primary School

MILLENNIUM

M illennium Bug is coming,
I n the year 2000.
L ights shining in the street,
L ots of people out to meet.
E veryone dancing,
N ear midnight celebrating.
N ew year is coming,
I t is a minute to midnight,
U niverse is shouting,
M illennium is here!

Nicola Wilkinson (10)
Sudbrook Primary School

MILLENNIUM

C enturies have passed,
E vents come and go.
L ights are glittering,
E urope is celebrating.
B ritain is changing,
R ivers are rising.
A lso weather's changing.
T rees have been burnt.
I nfants, getting smarter.
N o one's outside.
G round is shaken.

A new start.

N ew cars, water powered.
E clipses will happen.
W eather will be worse.

M illennium Dome is new.
I mproving money.
L ots of new buildings.
L abour see the day!
E uro is near.
N ew things to do.
N ew beginnings.
I mportant meetings.
U nderground houses.
M illennium is here!

James McConnell (10)
Sudbrook Primary School

MILLENNIUM

M illennium time is here,
I t will be good.
L ook at the Dome.
L ike the Dome or not.
E clipse in August.
N ew games,
N ew lights,
I 'm in the millennium house.
U se the lights for pictures,
M illennium Bug is here!

Jonathan Cave (10)
Sudbrook Primary School

MILLENNIUM

M aking a poem,
I nteresting events.
L isten to the music,
L ook at people having fun.
E vening celebrations,
N ew year is here!
N ow let's celebrate.
I n the night get drunk,
U ncle's celebrating.
M illennium 2000 is here!

Ben Brown (10)
Sudbrook Primary School

MILLENNIUM

M illennium Bug
I s coming.
L ights turn to dark.
L ife is different.
E clipse in August.
N ew year celebrations.
N ew homes.
I nteresting things.
U K in the Euro.
M illennium Dome.

Joe Roberts (11)
Sudbrook Primary School

MILLENNIUM

M eet your friends at night,
I t is so fascinating.
L iving in the future,
L iving in underground homes.
E ducation is better,
N ature is beautiful.
N ature is wonderful,
I nternet is really good.
U nderneath the ground we live,
M illennium Dome!

David Chandler (11)
Sudbrook Primary School

MILLENNIUM

Millennium is here,
I would like to see,
Living in the future,
Eclipse in August too.

New year celebration,
No one's at home.
Imagining the future,
Of the New Year's Dome!

Packing, queuing,
Waiting to get in,
For all the amazing things,
They are going to see.

The human body,
They have built.
Art, paintings, other things.
It is so great!

Carly Lauran Thompson (10)
Sudbrook Primary School

MILLENNIUM

My underground house
Is funny to some,
Laughing and laughing
Until the day's done.

There's something in my mind,
That will be a while,
It changes my face
From a frown to a smile.

The Millennium Dome!
It's big, it's round,
Thousands of tourists,
London's where it's found.

Packing and queuing,
Waiting to see
The things that amaze,
Both you and me.

Gary Smith (10)
Sudbrook Primary School

MILLENNIUM

In the year 2000
There's a Millennium Bug,
A Millennium Bug
In the year 2000.

In the Millennium Dome
There's a work zone,
And a body zone too
In the Millennium Dome.

In the body zone
You see lungs
Of someone who's smoked
And also their bones.

In the work zone
There are skilful games,
And the key to your future
Is in the work zone.

Joe Underwood (11)
Sudbrook Primary School

MILLENNIUM

M eet the 21st century, say goodbye to the 20th century,
I t will be so exciting looking forward.
L ife may change.
L ife may get better.
E veryone should care for the Earth.
N ew ideas.
N ew inventions.
I am looking forward to vehicles of the future,
U niting everyone around the world.
M aking the most of a new start.

Adam Faulkner (11)
Sudbrook Primary School

MILLENNIUM

M y mum is happy,
I am too,
L iving in the future.
L earning too,
E arning as well,
N an's having a party,
N atalie's not well.
I an's new football.
U ncle is giving presents.
M illennium Dome.

David Morgan (10)
Sudbrook Primary School

EDDY KENNING

Teacher yeller,
Good smeller.
Big eater,
Double seater.
Hates Dramer
Is a farmer.
Dog liker,
Bad biker.
Tractor rider
Loves cider.
Quad winner
Likes dinner.
Hunter caller,
OK footballer.

Richard Clarke (11)
Tutshill CE Primary School

DREAMING

I saw a shocking pink pig walk on the moon.
I saw a fish as big as a ship.
I saw a red, red apple with a brown pip.
I saw a man with a broken hip.
I saw a cat on a beautiful rainbow.
I saw a lion roar at a mouse.
I saw a tree grow in the sun.
I saw a raindrop twinkle on a flower.
I saw a spider drop from a cloud.
I saw the glistening sun in the sky.

Kaylee Bains (10)
Tutshill CE Primary School

MY NAN (I THINK)

Nail perfecter
bargain detector
     penguin walker
     window gawper
hair redder
deep bedder
     bright dresser
     make-up messer
ultra-glow lover
Apollo's cover
     school embarrasser
     shop browser
aisle singer
wrinkly finger
     scarf wearer
     daughter carer
broad waver
leg shaver

That's my nan down to a tee
so please, please, please help me!

Chloe Martin (10)
Tutshill CE Primary School

TWINKLE, TWINKLE

Twinkle, twinkle little cat,
sitting down on the mat.
Up above the world you jump,
you're sure to land with a bump.
Twinkle, twinkle little cat,
sitting down on the mat.

Twinkle, twinkle little dog,
chasing a baby frog.
Round the roundabout you run,
You must be having great fun.
Twinkle, twinkle little dog
chasing a baby frog.

Katie Smith (9)
Tutshill CE Primary School

WRITTEN IN SUMMER

The peacock is chatting,
The puddles do glitter.
The lakes are battering,
The red breast robin's song is bitter,
The puddles do glitter.
   The dark green fields rest in the sun.
The oldest and youngest
Are hard at work with the strongest muscles.
The geese go waddle, waddle,
Their feet never paddle.
   There are forty paddling like each other.
Like an army fighting and biting.
Like a blizzard biting and lighting
And now on a pill on top of a hill,
   The old fogy with a bogy saying, 'Anon-anon.'
There is gloom in the tomb
Where the tomb goes *boom!*
Small puffy clouds go whooshing by
When the blue sky never says, 'Bye.'

Kelly Duncan (9)
Tutshill CE Primary School

MARS

Mars the planet,
red and hot,
reminds me of people getting shot.
In the future it can gaze,
space is like some horrible maze.

Mars the planet,
with no life,
reminds me of a blood-stained knife.
Something like a big, big war,
there is danger I am sure.

Mars the planet,
with shooting stars,
UFOs like all our cars.
Very beautiful and unique,
I bet it would be an antique.

Robert Jones (10)
Tutshill CE Primary School

MUSIC

I love playing music, piano and recorder.
I've got a piano but I didn't know I could afford her.
I play A, B & C
All the way up to G.
That's as far as music goes
With pressing and plucking and using bows.
C, D, A, B, G
I play music happily
B, D, C, F, A
I have played that twice today.

Sophie McRoberts (9)
Tutshill CE Primary School

DREAMING

I saw a dog talk to a cat.
I saw a horse with a polka dot hat.
I saw a butterfly land on the sun.
I saw an elephant give a boy a bun.
I saw a monkey swimming the channel.
I saw a giraffe wearing my flannel.
I saw a gorilla eating a man.
I saw an alien in a can.
I saw a rainbow, black as night.
I saw black, shining bright.
I saw a jellybean on a trampoline.
I saw a world with no one being *mean!*

Kristina Ellen Connolly (10)
Tutshill CE Primary School

KENNING SCHOOL

Maths puzzler
Food guzzler
Assembly killer
Paint spiller
Lunchtime griller
Teacher brainer
Child learner
PE dancer
Dinner clasher
Children natter
Teachers chatter
Cleaner shimmer
Workmen hammer.

Harriet Lewis (10)
Tutshill CE Primary School

THE UNKNOWN BEACH

It's hot and cool in this place,
Palm trees waving in the cool breeze,
Fish slither around in the water,
Glistening in the sun.
Shadows everywhere making us tall,
Sand yellow brushing on the floor,
Cool drinks, ice-creams melting in the sun,
Sky blue, blue as the sea,
Sun as orange as a felt-tip pen,
Shorts wearing on your bare legs,
Too hot for playing games,
Suncream to protect you from burning,
Eating out on summer evenings,
Swimming in the warm, clear water,
No one comes here, it's just so beautiful.

Tristesse Hawker (11)
Tutshill CE Primary School

MARS' ALIENS

Aliens decapitating,
Aliens terror creating.
An alien brings out a knife,
An alien brings war and strife.
Intelligent technology,
Some dark, evil witchcraftory.
Aliens are human killing,
Aliens they are blood spilling.

Tommy Edwards (11)
Tutshill CE Primary School

MY NAN

Bargain hunter,
Shop punter.
Hair reflector,
Stripe detector.
Hair bleacher,
Big feature.
Purple dresser,
Hair messer.
Man stalker,
Garden gawper.
Old nutter,
Head butter.
Child stresser,
Everything messer!

That's my nan down to the toe,
Now you know she's my foe!

Lyndsey Connolly (10)
Tutshill CE Primary School

MARS!

Mars is power.
Mars is red, hot, full of danger.
Mars is a huge, red round ball wandering in the solar system.
Mars is full of life waiting to burst out.
Mars is dry and hot.
Mars is all on its own.
Mars is a fresh, juicy apple.

Ashvin Nair (10)
Tutshill CE Primary School

MY HORSE

My horse is Bay,
a lot to pay.
Very lovely
and cuddly!

My horse her name is Shantih,
up the hill she's always panty!
Galloping across the moors
on all fours.

My horse, I'll never let her go,
and so,
she'll stay with me,
like a pod and a pea!

Heather Leighton (10)
Tutshill CE Primary School

MARS

The planet Mars
out in space.
Big and red
like an embarrassed face.
Giving out its warning
to keep away.
Strong, proud and hot.
Thick misty clouds covering the surface.
Twinkling stars that move by it.

Aimee Townshend (10)
Tutshill CE Primary School

MARS IS WAR

M any aliens rising for war.
A liens are ready. Ready for death.
R ising from beneath the cracks.
S ay they, 'There will be no surrendering!'

I nto the warships.
S liding their claws on to the warships' control pads.

W anting to win, wanting to be triumphant.
A s they fly, aliens die.
R oar they, 'I will not die!'

Tristan Truran (10)
Tutshill CE Primary School

MARS ENDING

Mars is hot
as a sauna,
red as an apple
speeding through the sky.

Everyone is dying.
No one is crying.
Dying, dying,
I'm dying.
Now everyone is in bed,
Going to the living dead.

Katie Szmaglik (11)
Tutshill CE Primary School

Mars Attacks!

M ars is so dull and hardly any colour
A nd maybe has aliens all over.
R ound and round,
S aturn, Earth then Mars.

A fter sun sets on Mars, spaceships rise on Mars.
T ears may float in the air,
T all or they may be small.
A fternoon on Earth may mean bedtime on Mars.
C locks may strike an hour early or late.
K eep that Mars' dust, might change one day,
S o look out there!

Justin Fisher (11)
Tutshill CE Primary School

Reminds Me Of My Dad!

I know a boy with a grin so cheeky,
When I see his face he looks rather sneaky.
His hair is so curly and very frizzy,
It must have made his barber dizzy.
A fat little boy with dimples on his knees,
Who is very like a teddy bear you would like to squeeze.
His shirt front bulges over his tum,
And threatens to send the buttons to the sun.
Face goes bright red when he's mad,
This reminds me of my dad!

Amy Beavis (10)
Tutshill CE Primary School

COFFIN ALERT

Lying in my coffin
knowing I'm not dead.
Knocking on the roof,
'Open up!' I said.

Lying in the darkness,
knowing I can't move.
Nothing here to play with
no radio or food.

Armpits getting smelly,
'I need the loo quick!'
Great, that is all I need,
Now I feel sick.

Smell of wee is rising,
I'm blowing up inside.
'Open up,' I cried once more,
'Ya know I'm still alive.'

One year later in my coffin,
this time I am dead.
Rotting away into the ground
wish I was alive instead!

Rebecca Goatman (11)
Tutshill CE Primary School

ALIENS

Aliens have landed
with seventeen eyes.
They could be dangerous,
they could be spies.
They have sharp red teeth,
an enormous nose -
Oh look, they've got no toes.
They have little bodies
and can fly.
Hey everyone, we're gonna die.
The aliens just wanted to say hello,
they've come, they've been and now they go.
They left behind a laser gun,
now I can zap people, just for fun.

Lucy Stewart (11)
Tutshill CE Primary School

THE BORING VICTORIANS

'It's not amusing,' the Victorians said.
But they invented pencil lead.
It makes a horrible sound on the chalk board.
How could they get around, I would be so bored.
Now we've invented a Ford.
But in those days when Victoria was queen,
the people were bad, cruel and mean.

Philip Simpson (10)
Tutshill CE Primary School

DREAMING

I saw the sun bright glitter in the sky.
I saw a man eating a pie on the moon.
I saw a spider fall from a clock.
I saw an ant sitting by the river having a smoke.
I saw a bee jumping up and down.
I saw a horse on a cloud.
I saw sea bull charge at a bird.
I saw a bright brown apple with a green pip.
I saw some pink milk make the tea turn rainbow bright.
I saw a baby sleep in the sky.
I saw a bright green melon as big as me.
I saw a child on a pink horse.
I saw a rocket landing on an orange.
I saw a bear drinking beer.

Heather Cameron (10)
Tutshill CE Primary School

I'VE NEVER SPIED

I've never spied a witch on a bus,
or cats and dogs wearing fancy stuff.
Then worst of them all
a bunny rabbit on a stall.

I've never spied a purple cat,
wearing a big pink hat
and when I went to the zoo
I never spied a giraffe on the loo.

Christopher Williams (10)
Tutshill CE Primary School

FARM ANIMALS

Farm animals, farm animals all over the farm.
Animals, animals do not do much harm.
Over here and over there
just take a lot of care.

Horses are used for pulling things,
you make them pull a king.
Jumping, jumping over logs,
even running in the fog.

Baby lambs running around,
baby pups always pounding.
Baby calves standing still,
baby piglets by the mill.

Sarah Bradley (9)
Tutshill CE Primary School

MILLENNIUM MUSIC!

Millennium music playing through the town.
It will go down the street, down, down, down.
Millennium music goes here and there
It plays through your ears and down the stair.
Millennium music going down hills,
It plays through buildings and windmills.

You'll see the notes float by and hear them play a tune.
You'll see them by the sun and see them by the moon.
You'll see them float across the sparkling stars
But they could do a lot of damage maybe involving cars.

Serena Corbin (9)
Tutshill CE Primary School

COLOURED FOOD

Yellow bananas, purple plums, red tomatoes, black chocolate.
Slice it in a tick.
Say it quick.

Yellow bananas, purple plums, red tomatoes, black chocolate.
Add the pasta.
Say it fasta.

Yellow bananas, purple plums, red tomatoes, black chocolate.
Now repeat it
while you eat it.

Yellow bananas, purple plums, red tomatoes, black chocolate.
Yuck.
Tastes disgusting!

Natasha Cubbin (10)
Tutshill CE Primary School

TELEVISION

T V takes up most of my day.
E mmerdale, Neighbours, Home and Away.
L ive and Kicking, Blue Peter too.
E astenders, Rugrats and Havakazoo.
V icar of Dibley, The News and ET
I simply love them, turn on the TV.
S mart, The Simpsons are really just fine.
I watch them sometimes 'til half past nine.
O Zone, Grange Hill, Barney and Me.
N ewsround is next, but it's time for my tea.

Jessica Hollies (9)
Tutshill CE Primary School

THE CHOCOLATE MOOSE

The friendly moose with chocolate skin
I love him with my heart.
I try to take him to the park
but he can't fit in my cart.

He wanders through the house
not knowing what to do.
I wish I was home to play with you
'cause I'm stuck here in the loo.

I imagine him in the mountains
but I prefer him here.
I see him drinking from fountains
it all becomes so clear.

Freya Mills (9)
Tutshill CE Primary School

MILLENNIUM NONSENSE

M etal machines.
I   ncredible acts.
L ong cars.
L ovely and cute new animals.
E lectric cars.
N ew games.
N ew babies.
I   visible cars.
U gly boys.
M onkeys that talk.

Gemma Duncan (8)
Tutshill CE Primary School

DISNEYLAND PARIS

D isneyland is a lot of fun.
I f you want to skip the queue you'd better run.
S leeping Beauty's castle awaits you as you go in.
N o one hates it fat or thin.
E veryone loves the rides there.
Y ou would like it even better than a funfair.
L oads of people go to stay
A nd if you do you'll not want to go away.
N early everyone has a hug from Mickey Mouse.
D on't miss the haunted house.

P retty Minnie will hug you too.
A ll the pirates are attacking, make sure that they don't catch you.
R ain or shine, it'll be great
I t's really good it shuts at eight.
S o make sure you go there for your holidays.

Alice Workman (9)
Tutshill CE Primary School

I DON'T LIKE YOU!

If I were a snake
and you were a frog
I'd be most careful around the lake
not to bite you, the rat or the dog.

If I were a frog and you were a snake,
it wouldn't be like that
you would disturb the lake
and would bite me, the dog and the rat.

Sarah Parsons (9)
Tutshill CE Primary School

FOOTBALL GLORY

F ootball is cool.
O vermars is not a fool.
O vermars does not play pool.
T he striker has a part to play,
B urgers are what they eat all day.
A t the back he'll always stay.
L uis Ronaldo the best all May.
L uis Ronaldo the best all day.

G ianfranco Zola could be the best.
L eaving would be a total mess.
O r Chelsea would be even worse.
R onaldo is way better than me.
Y et again another beat me.

Alex Compton (8)
Tutshill CE Primary School

ALL THINGS SMALL AND SMELLY

All things small and smelly,
The small red ant that bites.
They have such brutish venom
Like scorpions that fight.

All things small and slimy,
The creatures large and hairy.
The little wasp that painfully stings.
Are they really that scary?

Matthew Newell (9)
Tutshill CE Primary School

I REMEMBER

I remember, I remember,
the hospital big and black, also my first smack.
The country big and high almost in the sky.

I remember, I remember,
my house up a hill, before I moved to Tutshill.
The bridge with one rock, rather rocked.
The school that I went to, it had two big fences.

I remember, I remember,
the water crystal-clear which went to a forest very near.
The forest is big with mud which stinks and sinks.

I remember, I remember,
the snow white and wet.
Then the year started again.

Alex Pritchard (8)
Tutshill CE Primary School

FOOTBALL CRAZY

F ifty more minutes to go.
O ff we go
O n to the pitch
T aking place in goal
B ringing the football to the pitch
A t last the other team is here
L onging, hoping that we win
L east we won the FA Cup.

Emma Childs (9)
Tutshill CE Primary School

NEW YEAR'S EVE 2000

I think the world will break in half.
The sun will come too close
and we shall al be burned to shreds,
probably in our beds.

I will survive and hopefully all my friends
but even if we did survive we all die in the end.
The volcanoes will blow, the seas will be dry,
but only I shall be left on an island under no sky.

The two parts of the Earth will float away,
through the Milky Way.
That's what I think will happen
on that dreaded day.

Rosalind Jacks (9)
Tutshill CE Primary School

THE COOLEST MAN IN TOWN

There was this coolest man in town
and he never used to frown.
He always went abroad, that's how he got brown.
He was full of funk,
and the ladies thought he was a hunk!
With his jobs,
he had no probs.

There was this coolest man in town,
he knew every noun!
Everyone thought he was the king,
everywhere he would always sing!
There was this coolest man in town . . .

Verity Gatt (9)
Tutshill CE Primary School

THE PHEASANT ESCAPE

One sunny day.
There was a pheasant in a field.
There the pheasant lay
With the fences like a shield.

Then along came a butcher,
In his right hand a knife.
That butcher really wanted her,
This could be the end of her life.

The pheasant ducked,
The butcher thought of toasting
Or how about plucking
But he decided roasting.

Michael Duke (8)
Tutshill CE Primary School

THE CAT THAT HAD A TALL HAT

There was a cat that lost his hat.
He looked under the mat it still wasn't there.
He sat on the sofa , he felt a point
but it wasn't a hat.
He looked on the mat and he felt the hat.

Catherine Keenan (8)
Tutshill CE Primary School

THE HEDGEHOG IN THE GARDEN

A little brown hedgehog,
His spikes are very sharp
Under a pile of leaves.
Daytime goes while he sleeps,
At night he eats snails, beetles or bugs.

Anita Dewhurst (10)
Tutshill CE Primary School

CHEETAH

Peter wanted to meet a cheetah.
Peter wanted to race against a cheetah.
But the cheetah beat-a Peter.
Peter said, 'Pleased to meet ya!'

Dominic White (9)
Tutshill CE Primary School

DREAMS

I saw a pig fly over the moon
I saw a real man in a cartoon
I saw a car drive along with one tyre
I saw a fish curled up by the fire.
I saw a giant the size of a mouse
I saw an orange the size of a house
I saw a lemon that tasted like sweets
I saw a still object running down the streets
I saw an ant overtake a galloping horse
I saw a toad with skin that was coarse
I saw a mouse pouncing on a cat
I saw a tall tree as high as a mat
I saw a cricket hop over the moon
I saw an elephant the size of a spoon
I saw a broken object mend
I see this poem coming to an end.

Ruth Mercer (11)
Tutshill CE Primary School

WINDOW

Look through a window what will you see next?
A transparent door to your imagination
Out of it you can see anything,
Watch the world change as it happens,
You can see peoples' lives before you and not even notice
People getting killed, people falling in love.
It's a gate to the outside world,
You never know what you'll see through your window.

Ben Jones (11)
Tutshill CE Primary School